The
Teacher's Daybook

JIM BURKE

2012–2013

HEINEMANN

Portsmouth, NH

Heinemann
361 Hanover Street
Portsmouth, NH 03801–3912
www.heinemann.com

Offices and agents throughout the world

The author and publisher wish to thank those who have generously given permission to reprint borrowed material:

"Five Core Propositions" reprinted with permission from the National Board for Professional Teaching Standards, www.nbpts.org. All rights reserved.

Personal and Professional Needs Assessment Form adapted from Michael Osborn and Suzanne Osborn, *Public Speaking, Fourth Edition*. Copyright © 1997 by Houghton Mifflin Company. Reprinted with permission.

Library of Congress Cataloging-in-Publication Data
Burke, Jim
    The teacher's daybook, 2012–2013 : time to teach, time to learn, time to live / Jim Burke
      p. cm.
    Includes bibliographical references.
    ISBN-13: 978-0-325-04222-0
    ISBN-10: 0-325-04222-5
    1. Teaching—Aids and devices. 2. Education—Calendars. 3. Education—Forms. I. Title.

LB1044.88 B87 2002
371.3—dc21   2002011669

Editor: Tobey Antao
Production: Patricia Adams
Composition: Kim Arney
Interior and cover design: Lisa Fowler
Manufacturing: Steve Bernier

Printed in the United States of America on acid-free paper
16   15   14   13   12   VP   1   2   3   4   5

SOME OF THE FORMS NOW AVAILABLE ON THE WEBSITE

The Teacher's Daybook by Jim Burke (Heinemann: Portsmouth, NH); © 2012 by Jim Burke.

In a conversation there is always more than one voice, and one of the voices must be our own or it is no conversation at all.

—David Whyte, from *Crossing the Unknown Sea: Work as a Pilgrimage of Identity*

The Teacher's Daybook offers you a useful resource to help you keep track of information and plan your lessons. This is why I originally created it. What I soon realized, however, was that it was not only a planner but an invitation, one I had unwittingly extended to myself and the thousands of colleagues who have joined the community of *Daybook* users since I first created it in 2002. An invitation to what? To join a conversation—with ourselves, each other, and our profession—about the meaning and challenges of our work, but also about our needs apart from that work. As Parker Palmer says in *The Courage to Teach*, "the personal can never be divorced from the professional . . . [for] we teach who we are" (1998, xi).

In the intervening years, my own "Circle of Friends," a concept *The Teacher's Daybook* explores throughout the year, has grown into a community that has not only enriched my life and teaching, but also improved the *Daybook* itself. I have traveled around the country, meeting and speaking with teachers, new and experienced , suburban and urban, public and private, about our work. On a lovely evening in Monterey, at a beautiful retreat center on the coast, we gathered in a circle with the poet David Whyte as our guest, to discuss our conceptions of work and hear David read poems in his remarkable Irish way. There we met for several days, using our *Daybooks* to guide us through a series of reflections as the new school year began. On another occasion, the *Daybook* brought me into conversation with hundreds of beleaguered public school teachers in Chicago, whose administrators decided the teachers, more than anything else, needed the chance to enter into the conversation with themselves and each other about both their personal and professional lives so they could meet the demands of the year ahead with the courage and strength our work requires. For several years, Vicki Spandel and I ran a summer retreat called "Reading, Writing, and You," in wonderful places that allowed for a sense of escape. Everyone received a *Daybook* and began each day with a morning session of reflection and discussion (along with a delicious breakfast, of course!). In more recent years, it is new and student-teachers who have increasingly joined the conversation, seeking through *The Teacher's Daybook* and our discussions a sense of clarity about their work and the courage to meet the demands it places upon us all, but them in particular. On a more personal level, *The Teacher's Daybook* has brought me into conversation with Parker Palmer, Sam Intrator, and Don Graves, all of whom have become, through our friendship, their guidance, and their books, my mentors. Their ideas, as well as our conversations about teachers' personal and professional lives, infuse this book and inform my own use of it.

Don Graves, whose book *The Energy to Teach* (2001) transformed much of my thinking about reflection, taught me the value of even five minutes of writing. On the Weekly Planning pages, you will find space to think about your week, something I find essential to my own personal and professional health. Such reflection calls to mind so many of the ideas I have learned from Parker Palmer, whose book *The Courage to Teach: Exploring the Inner Landscape of a Teacher's Life* (1998) arguably began the movement toward introspection within the teaching profession. Parker often uses the analogy of the farmers of the Great Plains when discussing the demands on teachers' lives. During blizzards, these farmers would tie one end of a rope around their waist then tie the other end to their barn door before heading out to rescue their cattle stranded in a blizzard. For myself and many others, *The Teacher's Daybook* has become the rope that helps us find our way through the blizzard of demands we encounter in both our personal and professional lives. It is through such conversations that I can find my way back, not only to my home and family, but to the core values that led me to teaching in the first place. As David Whyte has written, "Work is where we can make ourselves; work is where we can break ourselves" (2001, 12). Whyte goes on to say of work that "good work is work that makes sense, and that grants sense and meaning to the one who is doing it and to those affected by it" (13).

It is this idea, that our work should make sense, that sums up the greatest threat to so many of us these days. We came into the classroom for a reason, with a sense of vocation that we too often find ourselves struggling to pursue due to the barrage of testing and interruptions that threaten the integrity of the story we want our work—and our lives—to tell. The challenges of our work are enough in and of themselves, but our personal lives merit just as much care and consideration. Every day I hear teachers speak of the demands of caring for aging parents or sick family members. Others talk openly, often with a tone of weariness in their voice, of the demands of caring for children, spouses, or parents who are suffering from serious illnesses such as cancer; others struggle to cope with these illnesses themselves, wondering how they can receive treatment and teach a full load at the same time, and yet they often must if they are to provide for their families. Listening to my colleagues and those in my Circle of Friends, I have come to the conclusion that if we do not feel well we cannot teach well, at least not for a sustained period of time.

I have been a public school teacher for eighteen years and plan to be one for many more to come. I have a wonderful wife and three great children, each of whom I love despite all the trouble that comes with each developmental stage. My mother ages and my mother-in-law now lives with us. My classes are always too large, the periods never quite long enough. Yet every Sunday evening I sit down with a cup of coffee, pull out my *Daybook*, and take time to reflect on the week to come and the one just past. My *Daybook* invites me to ask what matters most and to organize my time around those priorities. *The Teacher's Daybook* allows me to realize that I have not placed family first in the "Honor Your Roles" section for weeks, and at least forces me to confront that, extends the invitation to make room for it, and urges me to take concrete steps by making a reservation for dinner, going to a basketball game with my sons, or just walking my daughter Nora to her dance class down the street. It reminds me, too, to

reach out to one of my most cherished Circle of Friends, which is small but dear to me: Rebecca and Sandy, one a Special Education teacher, the other an ESL teacher, the three of us having long ago forged a bond through our work with struggling students. Every three months or so we go to the same small restaurant in San Francisco, treat ourselves to a delicious meal, and talk about books, life, gardening, children, and work.

Such conversations, as well as those I have had over the years with other colleagues and the greater community of *Daybook* users, keep the rope firmly cinched around my waist, allowing me to move between work and home, the personal and professional, without getting lost. This new edition of *The Teacher's Daybook* is an extension of those conversations and the *Daybook* community. While I often hear from people who read my other books, *Daybook* users write with specific requests about how to improve it. This is a book we have, ultimately, created together over the years. Here you will discover features including a full twelve-month planner with both monthly and weekly pages, all of them dated for the year to come.

I encourage you to let me know how I can improve the *Daybook* still more. Simply write to me at jburke@ englishcompanion.com and let me know your ideas.

In the meantime, enjoy your *Daybook*. More importantly, though, enjoy your work—and your life. Nothing will keep you alive to your work more than having a good and interesting life outside of it. Let *The Teacher's Daybook* be an invitation to begin the conversation with yourself, and let yourself not only make time to have that conversation but muster the courage needed to listen to that one voice you must develop, protect, or discover all over: your own.

The National Board for Professional Teaching Standards: Five Core Propositions

The National Board for Professional Teaching Standards seeks to identify and recognize teachers who effectively enhance student learning and demonstrate the high level of knowledge, skills, abilities, and commitments reflected in the following five core propositions.

1 Teachers Are Committed to Students and Their Learning

Accomplished teachers are dedicated to making knowledge accessible to all students. They act on the belief that all students can learn. They treat students equitably, recognizing the individual differences that distinguish one student from another and taking account of these differences in their practice. They adjust their practice based on observation and knowledge of their students' interests, abilities, skills, knowledge, family circumstances, and peer relationships.

Accomplished teachers understand how students develop and learn. They incorporate the prevailing theories of cognition and intelligence in their practice. They are aware of the influence of context and culture on behavior. They develop students' cognitive capacity and their respect for learning. Equally important, they foster students' self-esteem, motivation, character, and civic responsibility and their respect for individual, cultural, religious, and racial differences.

2 Teachers Know the Subjects They Teach and How to Teach Those Subjects to Students

Accomplished teachers have a rich understanding of the subject(s) they teach and appreciate how knowledge in their subject is created, organized, linked to other disciplines, and applied to real-world settings. While faithfully representing the collective wisdom of our culture and upholding the value of disciplinary knowledge, they also develop the critical and analytical capacities of their students.

Accomplished teachers command specialized knowledge of how to convey and reveal subject matter to students. They are aware of the preconceptions and background knowledge that students typically bring to each subject and of strategies and instructional materials that can be of assistance. They understand where difficulties are likely to arise and modify their practice accordingly. Their instructional repertoire allows them to create multiple paths to the subjects they teach, and they are adept at teaching students how to pose and solve their own problems.

3 Teachers Are Responsible for Managing and Monitoring Student Learning

Accomplished teachers create, enrich, maintain, and alter instructional settings to capture and sustain the interest of their students and to make the most effective use of time. They also are adept at engaging students and adults to assist their teaching and at enlisting their colleagues' knowledge and expertise to complement their own. Accomplished teachers command a range of generic instructional techniques, know when each is appropriate, and can implement them as needed. They are as aware of ineffectual or damaging practice as they are devoted to elegant practice.

They know how to engage groups of students to ensure a disciplined learning environment and how to organize instruction to allow the schools' goals for students to be met. They are adept at setting norms for social interaction among students and between students and teachers. They understand how to motivate students to learn and how to maintain their interest even in the face of temporary failure.

Accomplished teachers can assess the progress of individual students as well as that of the class as a whole. They employ multiple methods for measuring student growth and understanding and can clearly explain student performance to parents.

4 Teachers Think Systematically About Their Practice and Learn from Experience

Accomplished teachers are models of educated persons, exemplifying the virtues they seek to inspire in students—curiosity, tolerance, honesty, fairness, respect for diversity, and appreciation of cultural differences—and the capacities that are prerequisites for intellectual growth: the ability to reason and take multiple perspectives, to be creative and take risks, and to adopt an experimental and problem-solving orientation.

Accomplished teachers draw on their knowledge of human development, subject matter and instruction, and their understanding of their students to make principled judgments about sound practice. Their decisions are not only grounded in the literature but also in their experience. They engage in lifelong learning, which they seek to encourage in their students.

Striving to strengthen their teaching, accomplished teachers critically examine their practice and seek to expand their repertoire, deepen their knowledge, sharpen their judgment, and adapt their teaching to new findings, ideas, and theories.

5 | Teachers Are Members of Learning Communities

Accomplished teachers contribute to the effectiveness of the school by working collaboratively with other professionals on instructional policy, curriculum development, and staff development. They can evaluate school progress and the allocation of school resources in light of their understanding of state and local educational objectives. They are knowledgeable about specialized school and community resources that can be engaged for their students' benefit and are skilled at employing such resources as needed.

Accomplished teachers find ways to work collaboratively and creatively with parents, engaging them productively in the work of the school.

Take a few minutes to respond to these standards. Consider, for example, focusing on one proposition that you find particularly meaningful, or that you need to address this year.

1. **What is the *Daybook* and what can it do for me?**
2. **How should I use my *Daybook*?**
3. **How can I maximize my *Daybook's* value and usefulness?**
4. **What is a Circle of Friends and how does it work?**
5. **What does the *Daybook* website offer me that the *Daybook* itself does not?**

1   What is the *Daybook* and what can it do for me?

The Teacher's Daybook will allow you to achieve balance between your personal and professional life by helping you:

- Identify and prioritize your different roles at home and work

- Get organized and stay that way through weekly Tips for Teachers

- Improve your teaching weekly with Tips for Teaching

- Design and implement standards-based lessons that meet all students' needs

- Keep track of students, data, and resources through tools included in the appendices. (These can also be downloaded from the *Daybook* website and formatted to meet your individual needs.)

- Maximize instructional time by showing you how to plan for the short and long term

- Create and sustain meaningful professional discussions with colleagues who are also committed to being successful and healthy teachers

- Develop an annual record of what you did, when you did it, and how you did it

- Gather all the different information you'll need throughout the year—test dates, meetings, extracurricular duties, access codes, passwords, and substitute records—in one place, called The Teacher's Homepage

- Save time by creating templates—e.g., for substitutes—once that can be used or adapted over and over to meet different needs

2   How should I use my *Daybook*?

Let me begin by talking briefly about why I created the *Daybook* and how I use mine. Every year I would wonder what I did the year before when I taught a certain book or unit. I had a great system for organizing lesson plans and assignments; however, it did not give me a picture of what the entire year was like. Also, some years I would think, "I've never been this wiped out before—what is going on this year?!" Finally, I would sit, as you inevitably do, in faculty meetings or department meetings and try to take in the barrage of dates, scores, tests, and other information and then just stop listening because I couldn't keep track of it all. I should add that I was drowning in other information: the growing number of access codes, user names, passwords, and websites, not to mention phone numbers, email addresses, and substitute days.

I wanted one place to keep all this data, so I created The Teacher's Homepage. I suggest you sit down at the beginning of each year and fill this in, updating what is new and copying what remains the same from the previous year. Next time someone asks for your school fax number, you'll know *where* it is if you don't remember *what* it is. And when you wonder how many substitute days you had in September, or how many you've taken so far, you will know, just as you will be able to remember who paid for those days if you are asked. While I don't want to think about them, the state and district tests we must give— which seem to grow in number and demands annually— can really mess up my curriculum if I don't plan ahead. By sitting down in front of the school's master calendar and jotting all those dates down early in the year, I can avoid trouble down the road.

Some years I seemed to accomplish more than others, a feeling that bothered me as I had the same number of days each year. The *Daybook's* monthly calendars, as well as its Planning Page and Yearlong Planner, help me see the Big Picture when planning a unit or even a semester. This ensures that I get to all the different aspects of the curriculum I think matter most; it also makes my curriculum more integrated and cohesive. Finally, it allows me to be sure I am incorporating the different standards into my curriculum over the course of the year.

This is how I use my *Daybook:* I sit down on Sunday and think about the week ahead. I begin by identifying the major demands at home and school so I know which roles are most important. I fill in the Honor Your Roles diagram. One week, "Writer" might be the most important role, followed by "Father," and "Husband," and then "Teacher." It changes every week for different reasons. Then I choose my focus and set my goals for the week. Before I move on, I double-check the monthly calendar and my Teacher's Homepage to make sure there are no visits from the counselor, special schedules, assemblies, or tests.

Now I am ready to sketch out my week. Because I have different preps, I divide my Weekly Planner pages into sections for each class. These are small, but adequate for this phase. I am not writing up my entire lesson plan; I am only sketching out what I think should happen. I am drafting the week's work. When I finish doing this, I write up the first day's actual lesson plan using the Teach by Design template. I create one of these for each class. Finally, I take these Daily Lesson Plan pages, and all handouts, and put them in a large binder on my podium so I'll have a complete record of what I planned for that week. I try to collect examples of student work afterward to add to that day's lesson plan and handouts; that way I can show the students next year what good work on any given assignment looks like.

When I get home on Monday, I revisit my *Daybook,* consider what happened that day and what I want to happen the rest of the week, and make my next lesson plan accordingly. I use the Teach by Design checklist to be sure I am covering all my bases and meeting the needs of all my students. Over time, it becomes a mental checklist, but still I like to have it there to keep me from getting lazy or cutting corners.

At week's end, I sit down and write that week's Weekly Reflection. It takes me ten minutes, which is reasonable. More important, it gives me a sense of closure to the week. I can celebrate what went well and acknowledge what went wrong. I can admit that I feel wiped out, talk about what I learned, or even complain about what my students didn't learn. This brief reflec-

tion always helps me out by revealing what I'm thinking and how I'm feeling about work and life.

3 | How can I maximize my *Daybook's* value and usefulness?

I keep my own *Daybook* in an attractive 1" binder. This helps me coordinate all my variously sized documents—grades, attendance, data, and lesson plans—in one place. The binder adds additional functionality to my own *Daybook* by allowing me to insert separate planner pages (from the *Daybook* website), blank paper, and important documents. My *Daybook* binder has a professional look, which I appreciate since this represents my professional life. I once kept all such papers in a nondescript binder, which was inadvertently thrown out by the janitor one day in an overzealous effort to recycle what he thought was a binder full of useless papers. So I like my *Daybook* portfolio to look like something no one would ever think of throwing out!

While creating the *Daybook,* I field-tested it with a wide array of teachers in all grade levels and subject areas. Thanks to the help of these fellow teachers, we generated a range of ways to personalize your *Daybook* to meet your own individual needs. Here are some of the most useful suggestions:

- Write only in pencil so you can erase and reuse space.
- Maximize space by using color codes, abbreviations, and symbols.
- Add personal pictures of family and friends.
- Use different sized and colored sticky notes in places, to make it easy to reuse that space.
- Add pocket pages and the like into your portfolio for additional storage.
- Jot down access codes and passwords (e.g., for copy machines, voice mail, email accounts, and the substitute request system) *under* sticky notes.
- Add adhesive divider tabs to different sections for improved navigation to those sections of the *Daybook* that you use most often.

4 | What is a Circle of Friends and how does it work?

Throughout the *Daybook,* specifically in the Conversation section of the Weekly Planner Pages, I refer to the Circle of Friends. The term makes sense to me, for it captures what we need: inclusion and that notion of a friend who shares your ideals, commitments, and sense of engagement. My own Circle of Friends includes several people at work, but two in particular: Sandy and Rebecca. Together we confess, laugh, learn, and share our personal and professional lives. We schedule times to meet for dinner, and seek one another out when we need the extra touch or guidance of a good friend. At my first school, where I learned the value of a Circle of Friends, the whole English department had dinner together once a month to discuss the books we taught; we figured the books should hold up under scrutiny and that such discussions would remind us why we taught these books in the first place. One other Circle of Friends I have includes the thousands of teachers on www.englishcompanion.ning.com (a social network I created for English teachers) with whom I communicate every night as we help each other try to do our work better the next day.

There are no specific guidelines or rules for a Circle of Friends. However, you might understand it best as a sort of book group that doesn't necessarily read books. Or you might think of it as a philosophical roundtable similar to the Socrates Café described in Christopher Phillips' book (2001) of the same name. Visit his website at www.philosopher.org for suggestions on how to run such a successful discussion group.

5 | What does the *Daybook* website offer me that the *Daybook* itself does not?

The companion website (books.heinemann.com/daybook) exists to help you work better and get the most use from your *Daybook.* The site offers:

- Links to useful sites and resources
- Downloadable versions of the *Daybook* pages you use most often and of which you want to have clean copies
- Additional forms, planner pages, and resources
- Suggestions and documents to help you get funding to buy a *Daybook* for everyone in your department, district, or school.

QUICK INFORMATION

SCHOOL AND DISTRICT OFFICE INFORMATION

SCHOOL ADDRESS ______________________________

MAIN PHONE ______________________________

DEPARTMENT PHONE ______________________________

SCHOOL FAX ______________________________

DEPARTMENT FAX ______________________________

SCHOOL EMAIL ______________________________

SCHOOL URL ______________________________

DISTRICT ADDRESS ______________________________

DISTRICT PHONE ______________________________

DISTRICT FAX ______________________________

DISTRICT URL ______________________________

SCHEDULE 1	SCHEDULE 2	SCHEDULE 3

	CLASS	ROOM	#Ss	AID/VOLUNTER
0°				
1°				
2°				
3°				
4°				
5°				
6°				
7°				
AS				

SPRING SEMESTER

	CLASS	ROOM	#Ss	AID/VOLUNTER
0°				
1°				
2°				
3°				
4°				
5°				
6°				
7°				
AS				

TESTING DATES

PASSWORDS

USERNAMES

SUBSTITUTE INFORMATION

SUBSTITUTES

SUB COORDINATOR ___________________

SUB SYSTEM PHONE ___________________

SUB SYSTEM URL ___________________

ID ___________________

PASSWORD ___________________

DATE(S)	REASON	CONFIRMATION #	DATE(S)	REASON	CONFIRMATION #

1. Who You Are

Use the diagram to identify all the different roles you play in your personal life (e.g., spouse, child, parent, etc.).

2. Rank the different roles from most (1) to least (10) important.

3. What You Want: Write your personal goal statement

This year I want to . . .

4. Why You Want It: Provide a rationale

I want to achieve this goal so I can . . .

5. How You'll Achieve It: Set a plan

To reach this goal, I will . . .

1.

2.

3.

6. What Will Help You: Identify allies and resources

The following can help me achieve my goal:

PEOPLE

1.

2.

3.

BOOKS

1.

2.

3.

ORGS/OTHER

1.

2.

3.

7. Assessment

I will know I reached my goal if . . .

Books I Want to Read

1.

2.

3.

Experiences I Want to Have

1.

2.

3.

4.

5.

Places I Want to Go/People I Want to See

1.

2.

3.

4.

5.

Things I Want to Do More

1.

2.

3.

4.

5.

Things I Want to Do Less (or Stop Doing)

1.

2.

3.

4.

5.

Things I Want to Learn About

1.

2.

3.

4.

5.

If I retired tomorrow, I would spend my time . . .

1. Who You Are

Use the diagram to identify all the different roles you play in your professional life this year (e.g., coach, teacher, mentor, etc.).

2. Rank the different roles from most (1) to least (10) important.

3. What You Want: Write your professional goal statement

This year I want to . . .

____

____

____

4. Why You Want It: Provide a rationale

I want to achieve this goal so I can . . .

____

____

5. How You'll Achieve It: Set a plan

To reach this goal, I will . . .

1. ____

2. ____

3. ____

6. What Will Help You: Identify allies and resources

The following can help me achieve my goal:

PEOPLE
1. ____
2. ____
3. ____

BOOKS
1. ____
2. ____
3. ____

ORGS/OTHER
1. ____
2. ____
3. ____

7. Assessment

I will know I've reached my goal if . . .

____

____

Professional Books I Want to Read

1. ____
2. ____
3. ____

Professional Experiences I Want to Have

1. ____
2. ____
3. ____
4. ____

New Subjects or Texts I Want to Teach

1. ____
2. ____
3. ____
4. ____

Contributions I Want to Make

1. ____
2. ____
3. ____
4. ____

Things I Want to Do Less (or Stop Doing)

1. ____
2. ____
3. ____
4. ____

Things I Want to Learn About

1. ____
2. ____
3. ____
4. ____

Write your own job description (based on the teacher you want to be):

____

____

____

____

2012

January

S	M	T	W	T	F	S
1	2	3	4	5	6	7
8	9	10	11	12	13	14
15	16	17	18	19	20	21
22	23	24	25	26	27	28
29	30	31				

February

S	M	T	W	T	F	S
			1	2	3	4
5	6	7	8	9	10	11
12	13	14	15	16	17	18
19	20	21	22	23	24	25
26	27	28	29			

March

S	M	T	W	T	F	S
				1	2	3
4	5	6	7	8	9	10
11	12	13	14	15	16	17
18	19	20	21	22	23	24
25	26	27	28	29	30	31

April

S	M	T	W	T	F	S
1	2	3	4	5	6	7
8	9	10	11	12	13	14
15	16	17	18	19	20	21
22	23	24	25	26	27	28
29	30					

May

S	M	T	W	T	F	S
		1	2	3	4	5
6	7	8	9	10	11	12
13	14	15	16	17	18	19
20	21	22	23	24	25	26
27	28	29	30	31		

June

S	M	T	W	T	F	S
					1	2
3	4	5	6	7	8	9
10	11	12	13	14	15	16
17	18	19	20	21	22	23
24	25	26	27	28	29	30

July

S	M	T	W	T	F	S
1	2	3	4	5	6	7
8	9	10	11	12	13	14
15	16	17	18	19	20	21
22	23	24	25	26	27	28
29	30	31				

August

S	M	T	W	T	F	S
			1	2	3	4
5	6	7	8	9	10	11
12	13	14	15	16	17	18
19	20	21	22	23	24	25
26	27	28	29	30	31	

September

S	M	T	W	T	F	S
						1
2	3	4	5	6	7	8
9	10	11	12	13	14	15
16	17	18	19	20	21	22
23	24	25	26	27	28	29
30						

October

S	M	T	W	T	F	S
	1	2	3	4	5	6
7	8	9	10	11	12	13
14	15	16	17	18	19	20
21	22	23	24	25	26	27
28	29	30	31			

November

S	M	T	W	T	F	S
				1	2	3
4	5	6	7	8	9	10
11	12	13	14	15	16	17
18	19	20	21	22	23	24
25	26	27	28	29	30	

December

S	M	T	W	T	F	S
						1
2	3	4	5	6	7	8
9	10	11	12	13	14	15
16	17	18	19	20	21	22
23	24	25	26	27	28	29
30	31					

2013

January

S	M	T	W	T	F	S
		1	2	3	4	5
6	7	8	9	10	11	12
13	14	15	16	17	18	19
20	21	22	23	24	25	26
27	28	29	30	31		

February

S	M	T	W	T	F	S
					1	2
3	4	5	6	7	8	9
10	11	12	13	14	15	16
17	18	19	20	21	22	23
24	25	26	27	28		

March

S	M	T	W	T	F	S
					1	2
3	4	5	6	7	8	9
10	11	12	13	14	15	16
17	18	19	20	21	22	23
24	25	26	27	28	29	30
31						

April

S	M	T	W	T	F	S
	1	2	3	4	5	6
7	8	9	10	11	12	13
14	15	16	17	18	19	20
21	22	23	24	25	26	27
28	29	30				

May

S	M	T	W	T	F	S
			1	2	3	4
5	6	7	8	9	10	11
12	13	14	15	16	17	18
19	20	21	22	23	24	25
26	27	28	29	30	31	

June

S	M	T	W	T	F	S
						1
2	3	4	5	6	7	8
9	10	11	12	13	14	15
16	17	18	19	20	21	22
23	24	25	26	27	28	29
30						

July

S	M	T	W	T	F	S
	1	2	3	4	5	6
7	8	9	10	11	12	13
14	15	16	17	18	19	20
21	22	23	24	25	26	27
28	29	30	31			

August

S	M	T	W	T	F	S
				1	2	3
4	5	6	7	8	9	10
11	12	13	14	15	16	17
18	19	20	21	22	23	24
25	26	27	28	29	30	31

September

S	M	T	W	T	F	S
1	2	3	4	5	6	7
8	9	10	11	12	13	14
15	16	17	18	19	20	21
22	23	24	25	26	27	28
29	30					

October

S	M	T	W	T	F	S
		1	2	3	4	5
6	7	8	9	10	11	12
13	14	15	16	17	18	19
20	21	22	23	24	25	26
27	28	29	30	31		

November

S	M	T	W	T	F	S
					1	2
3	4	5	6	7	8	9
10	11	12	13	14	15	16
17	18	19	20	21	22	23
24	25	26	27	28	29	30

December

S	M	T	W	T	F	S
1	2	3	4	5	6	7
8	9	10	11	12	13	14
15	16	17	18	19	20	21
22	23	24	25	26	27	28
29	30	31				

2014

January

S	M	T	W	T	F	S
			1	2	3	4
5	6	7	8	9	10	11
12	13	14	15	16	17	18
19	20	21	22	23	24	25
26	27	28	29	30	31	

February

S	M	T	W	T	F	S
						1
2	3	4	5	6	7	8
9	10	11	12	13	14	15
16	17	18	19	20	21	22
23	24	25	26	27	28	

March

S	M	T	W	T	F	S
						1
2	3	4	5	6	7	8
9	10	11	12	13	14	15
16	17	18	19	20	21	22
23	24	25	26	27	28	29
30	31					

April

S	M	T	W	T	F	S
		1	2	3	4	5
6	7	8	9	10	11	12
13	14	15	16	17	18	19
20	21	22	23	24	25	26
27	28	29	30			

May

S	M	T	W	T	F	S
				1	2	3
4	5	6	7	8	9	10
11	12	13	14	15	16	17
18	19	20	21	22	23	24
25	26	27	28	29	30	31

June

S	M	T	W	T	F	S
1	2	3	4	5	6	7
8	9	10	11	12	13	14
15	16	17	18	19	20	21
22	23	24	25	26	27	28
29	30					

July

S	M	T	W	T	F	S
		1	2	3	4	5
6	7	8	9	10	11	12
13	14	15	16	17	18	19
20	21	22	23	24	25	26
27	28	29	30	31		

August

S	M	T	W	T	F	S
					1	2
3	4	5	6	7	8	9
10	11	12	13	14	15	16
17	18	19	20	21	22	23
24	25	26	27	28	29	30
31						

September

S	M	T	W	T	F	S
	1	2	3	4	5	6
7	8	9	10	11	12	13
14	15	16	17	18	19	20
21	22	23	24	25	26	27
28	29	30				

October

S	M	T	W	T	F	S
			1	2	3	4
5	6	7	8	9	10	11
12	13	14	15	16	17	18
19	20	21	22	23	24	25
26	27	28	29	30	31	

November

S	M	T	W	T	F	S
						1
2	3	4	5	6	7	8
9	10	11	12	13	14	15
16	17	18	19	20	21	22
23	24	25	26	27	28	29
30						

December

S	M	T	W	T	F	S
	1	2	3	4	5	6
7	8	9	10	11	12	13
14	15	16	17	18	19	20
21	22	23	24	25	26	27
28	29	30	31			

Monthly Calendars

and

Weekly Calendars

NOTES/REMINDERS

SUNDAY	MONDAY	TUESDAY
5	6 CIVIC HOLIDAY (CANADA)	7
12	13	14
19	20	21
26	27	28

MONTHLY REFLECTION

WEDNESDAY	THURSDAY	FRIDAY	SATURDAY
1	2	3	4
8	9	10	11
15	16	17	18
22	23	24	25
29	30	31	

MONTHLY REFLECTION

September 2012

NOTES/REMINDERS	SUNDAY	MONDAY	TUESDAY
	2	**3** LABOR DAY	**4**
	9	**10**	**11** PATRIOT DAY
	16	**17** ROSH HASHANAH begins at sundown	**18**
	23/30	**24**	**25**

MONTHLY REFLECTION

WEDNESDAY	THURSDAY	FRIDAY	SATURDAY
			1
5	6	7	8
12	13	14	15
19	20	21	22 FALL EQUINOX
26 YOM KIPPUR begins at sundown	27	28	29

MONTHLY REFLECTION

MONTHLY PERSONAL GOAL

NOTES/REMINDERS

SUNDAY	MONDAY	TUESDAY
	1	2
7	8 COLUMBUS DAY	9
14	15	16
21	22	23
28	29	30

MONTHLY REFLECTION

The Teacher's Daybook by Jim Burke (Heinemann: Portsmouth, NH); © 2012 by Jim Burke.

WEDNESDAY	THURSDAY	FRIDAY	SATURDAY
3	4	5	6
10	11	12	13
17	18	19	20
24	25	26	27
31　HALLOWEEN			

MONTHLY REFLECTION

MONTHLY PERSONAL GOAL

NOTES/REMINDERS	SUNDAY	MONDAY	TUESDAY
	4 DAYLIGHT SAVINGS TIME ENDS	**5**	**6** ELECTION DAY
	11 VETERANS' DAY REMEMBERANCE DAY (CANADA)	**12**	**13**
	18	**19**	**20**
	25	**26**	**27**

MONTHLY REFLECTION

WEDNESDAY	THURSDAY	FRIDAY	SATURDAY
	1	2	3
7	8	9	10
14	15	16	17
21	22 THANKSGIVING	23	24
28	29	30	

MONTHLY REFLECTION

MONTHLY PERSONAL GOAL

NOTES/REMINDERS

SUNDAY	MONDAY	TUESDAY
2	**3**	**4**
9 HANUKKAH begins at sundown	**10**	**11**
16	**17**	**18**
23/30	**24/31** NEW YEAR'S EVE	**25** CHRISTMAS

MONTHLY REFLECTION

WEDNESDAY	THURSDAY	FRIDAY	SATURDAY
			1
5	6	7	8
12	13	14	15
19	20 WINTER SOLSTICE	21	22
26 KWANZAA BOXING DAY (CANADA)	27	28	29

MONTHLY REFLECTION

MONTHLY PERSONAL GOAL

NOTES/REMINDERS	SUNDAY	MONDAY	TUESDAY
			1 NEW YEAR'S DAY
	6	**7**	**8**
	13	**14**	**15**
	20	**21** MARTIN LUTHER KING, JR. DAY	**22**
	27	**28**	**29**

MONTHLY REFLECTION

The Teacher's Daybook by Jim Burke (Heinemann: Portsmouth, NH); © 2012 by Jim Burke.

WEDNESDAY	THURSDAY	FRIDAY	SATURDAY
2	3	4	5
9	10	11	12
16	17	18	19
23	24	25	26
30	31		

MONTHLY REFLECTION

MONTHLY PERSONAL GOAL

NOTES/REMINDERS

SUNDAY	MONDAY	TUESDAY
3	4	5
10 CHINESE NEW YEAR	11	12
17	18 PRESIDENT'S DAY	19
24	25	26

MONTHLY REFLECTION

The Teacher's Daybook by Jim Burke (Heinemann: Portsmouth, NH); © 2012 by Jim Burke.

WEDNESDAY	THURSDAY	FRIDAY	SATURDAY
		1	2 GROUNDHOG DAY
6	7	8	9
13	14 VALENTINE'S DAY	15	16
20	21	22	23
27	28		

MONTHLY REFLECTION

NOTES/REMINDERS

SUNDAY	MONDAY	TUESDAY
3	4	5
10 DAYLIGHT SAVINGS TIME BEGINS	11	12
17 ST. PATRICK'S DAY	18	19
24/31 EASTER	25	26 PASSOVER begins at sundown

MONTHLY REFLECTION

WEDNESDAY	THURSDAY	FRIDAY	SATURDAY
		1	2
6	7	8	9
13	14	15	16
20 SPRING EQUINOX	21	22	23
27	28	29 GOOD FRIDAY	30

MONTHLY REFLECTION

April 2013

NOTES/REMINDERS

SUNDAY	MONDAY	TUESDAY
	1	2
7	8	9
14	15	16
21	22 EARTH DAY	23
28	29	30

MONTHLY REFLECTION

WEDNESDAY	THURSDAY	FRIDAY	SATURDAY
3	4	5	6
10	11	12	13
17	18	19	20
24	25	26	27

MONTHLY REFLECTION

MONTHLY PERSONAL GOAL

NOTES/REMINDERS

SUNDAY	MONDAY	TUESDAY
5 CINCO DE MAYO	6	7
12 MOTHER'S DAY	13	14
19	20 VICTORIA DAY (CANADA)	21
26	27 MEMORIAL DAY	28

MONTHLY REFLECTION

WEDNESDAY	THURSDAY	FRIDAY	SATURDAY
1	2	3	4
8	9	10	11
15	16	17	18
22	23	24	25
29	30	31	

MONTHLY REFLECTION

NOTES/REMINDERS

SUNDAY	MONDAY	TUESDAY
2	3	4
9	10	11
16 FATHER'S DAY	17	18
23/30	24	25

MONTHLY REFLECTION

WEDNESDAY	THURSDAY	FRIDAY	SATURDAY
			1
5	6	7	8
12	13	14 FLAG DAY	15
19	20	21 SUMMER SOLSTICE	22
26	27	28	29

MONTHLY REFLECTION

MONTHLY PERSONAL GOAL

NOTES/REMINDERS	SUNDAY	MONDAY	TUESDAY
		1 CANADA DAY	**2**
	7	**8**	**9** RAMADAN
	14	**15**	**16**
	21	**22**	**23**
	28	**29**	**30**

MONTHLY REFLECTION

The Teacher's Daybook by Jim Burke (Heinemann: Portsmouth, NH); © 2012 by Jim Burke.

WEDNESDAY	THURSDAY	FRIDAY	SATURDAY
3	4 INDEPENDENCE DAY	5	6
10	11	12	13
17	18	19	20
24	25	26	27
31			

MONTHLY REFLECTION

PERSONAL

WEEKLY FOCUS:

WEEKLY GOAL:

PROFESSIONAL

WEEKLY FOCUS:

WEEKLY GOAL:

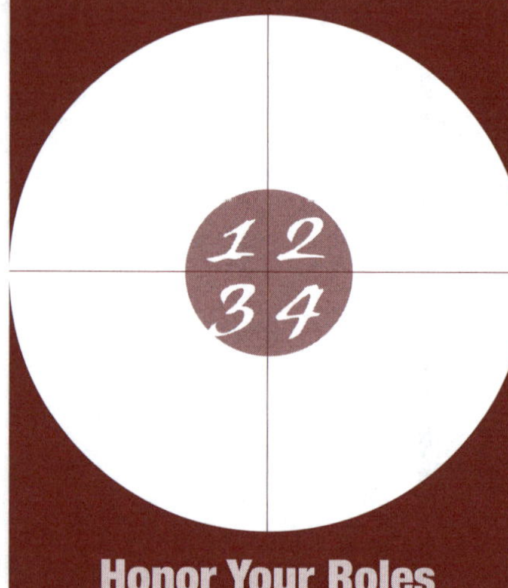

Honor Your Roles

TIPS FOR *Teachers*

Set up a student information system. Use the sheets in the *Daybook* Appendix to keep track of attendance and student information. Take a three-inch binder (to be referred to as the Master Binder) and create sections for whichever of the following are appropriate to your work: Lesson Plans, Roll, Grades, Masters (of certain frequently used handouts). Centralize all info; take this binder during any emergency (e.g., fire alarm).

TIPS FOR *Teaching*

Make the right first impression. Greet your students. Shake their hands. Smile. Communicate your high expectations and your commitment to help them all meet those expectations. Establish an atmosphere of respect for ideas, cultures, differences, and people. Reinforce these ideas through your own actions and assignments. Do whatever you must to ensure students leave class that first day/that first week thinking, "Wow, things are really going to happen in this class."

MONDAY 30

TUESDAY 31

WEDNESDAY 1

relax

TIPS FOR *Professional Learning*

JOIN THE CONVERSATION. Consider doing one of the following this year:

- Join (or start) a book group with friends or colleagues.
- Join an online or professional community for renewal and support.
- Set up a regular date with supportive, energetic colleagues; meet off campus at a nice place that allows for good conversation.
- Attend a professional conference or subscribe to a professional journal. If possible, include others so you can go together or discuss what you learn.
- Sign up for www.englishcompanion.ning.com.

Weekly Reflections

On a scale of 1–10, gauge (a) *how effective you were as a teacher this week, and* (b) *how you are feeling this week*. What adjective might best capture your teaching and your feelings this week?

THURSDAY 2

FRIDAY 3

REMINDERS · NOTES · WEEKEND HOMEWORK

plan ahead

- How does next week relate to this week?
- What continues to confuse or frustrate your students?
- Think of your class as a story: What should happen next?
- Who can help you be more successful next week?

PERSONAL

WEEKLY FOCUS:

WEEKLY GOAL:

PROFESSIONAL

WEEKLY FOCUS:

WEEKLY GOAL:

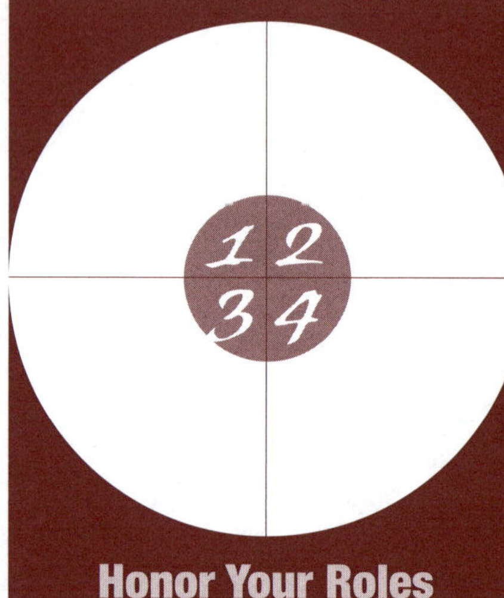

Honor Your Roles

TIPS FOR *Teachers*

Gather information. Enter into your Teacher's Homepage all scheduled meetings, classroom visits (e.g., by counselors), field trips, assemblies, emergency drills, and holidays. You can gather this information from your school's master calendar. It is a good idea to add to your Teacher's Homepage such logical information as video/resource pickup/drop-off days, district meetings, and important dates for applications, committees, and opportunities.

TIPS FOR *Teaching*

Establish a community of learners. Students should learn upon entering your room that you expect them to be readers and thinkers. Bring in books or magazines they will like. Ask someone who is reading a book to tell another person about it if the two have common interests. Foster a sense of community in the class that enables all students to give themselves permission to be learners, to take themselves and their interests seriously.

MONDAY 6

TUESDAY 7

WEDNESDAY 8

TIPS FOR *Professional Learning*

connect

CLASSROOM COMMUNITY. Kids cannot learn if they do not feel safe or welcome in a classroom. Ask colleagues what they do to achieve a safe environment. Consider making an effort to greet your students as they enter your classroom—and when you see them around school. Brainstorm other strategies with your Circle of Friends. Also, recall what some teachers did that made you feel at home in their class.

Weekly Reflections

On a scale of 1–10, gauge (a) *how effective you were as a teacher this week, and* (b) *how you are feeling this week*. What adjective might best capture your teaching and your feelings this week?

THURSDAY 9

FRIDAY 10

REMINDERS · NOTES · WEEKEND HOMEWORK

plan ahead

- How does next week relate to this week?
- What continues to confuse or frustrate your students?
- Think of your class as a story: What should happen next?
- Who can help you be more successful next week?

PERSONAL

WEEKLY FOCUS:

WEEKLY GOAL:

PROFESSIONAL

WEEKLY FOCUS:

WEEKLY GOAL:

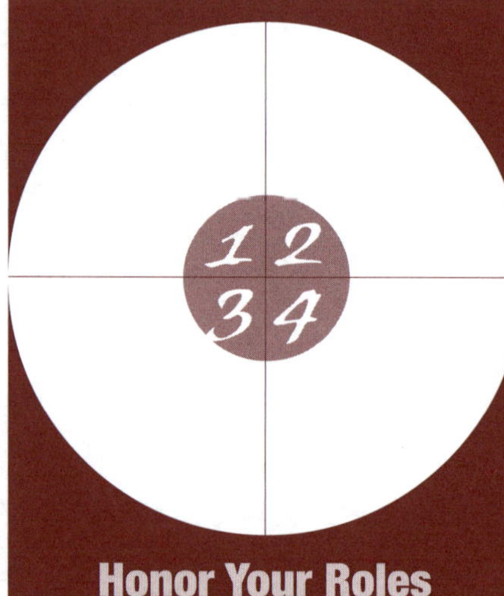

Honor Your Roles

TIPS FOR *Teachers*

Prepare for Back to School Night. Make available all materials students use in your classroom. Also post or organize a packet of core documents: prospectus, policies, rubrics, important dates, contact information. Consider writing parents a short letter in which you tell them what you have been doing and what is coming up. Let them know what they can do to help in the classroom or with events.

TIPS FOR *Teaching*

Create the conditions for effective learning. Students cannot succeed in an environment that will not support their learning. Environment in this case refers to not only the physical environment but the emotional and intellectual environment also. If students are to participate, engage, and learn, they must know they can take risks, feel safe, and have those materials their work requires. I realize we do not always have control over our physical environment; still, we do have control over the emotional and intellectual environment of our classes.

MONDAY 13

TUESDAY 14

WEDNESDAY 15

TIPS FOR *Professional Learning*

STUDY SUCCESS. When colleagues enjoy success with a student or a class—especially a difficult one—ask how they did it. If you work with people who seem to "do it all" or do it well, yet still have fun and remain healthy, ask how they do it. Ask them to join your Circle of Friends, where participants can share what they know and have learned about success. Such a conversation might begin by defining what "success" means for teachers—and students. A quick trip to www.morrisinstitute.com will provide useful ideas; there you can learn more about Tom Morris's "seven Cs" that lead to "true success."

Weekly Reflections

On a scale of 1–10, gauge (a) **how effective you were as a teacher this week, and** (b) **how you are feeling this week**. What adjective might best capture your teaching and your feelings this week?

THURSDAY 16

FRIDAY 17

REMINDERS · NOTES · WEEKEND HOMEWORK

plan ahead

▸ How does next week relate to this week?
▸ What continues to confuse or frustrate your students?
▸ Think of your class as a story: What should happen next?
▸ Who can help you be more successful next week?

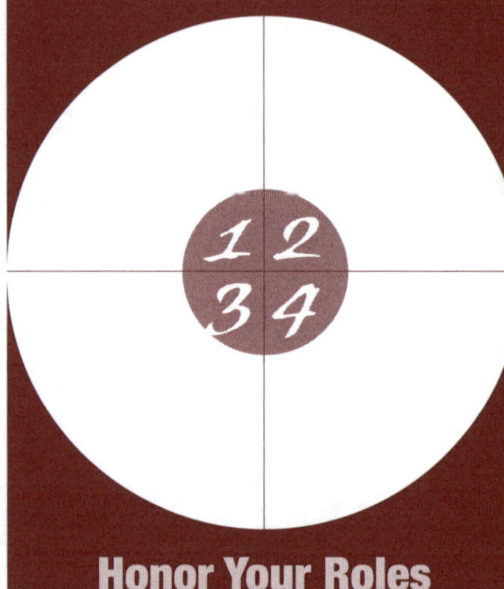

Honor Your Roles

TIPS FOR *Teachers*

Make your room your own. Not all teachers have their own room, of course. If you do, however, make a welcoming environment that celebrates kids and learning. Put up pictures and posters, student work and photographs, articles and artwork. See the Teacher's Checklist for more suggestions.

TIPS FOR *Teaching*

Read aloud to students. Reading aloud—by the students or the teacher—helps and engages readers of all ages. Hearing the text while looking at it on the page helps many readers process the information more effectively and also allows them to see how it should be read as they listen to the teacher's emphases and pauses and see how those accord with the punctuation and structure of the sentences.

MONDAY 20

TUESDAY 21

WEDNESDAY 22

The Teacher's Daybook by Jim Burke (Heinemann: Portsmouth, NH); © 2012 by Jim Burke.

TIPS FOR *Professional Learning*

PRINCIPLES OF TEACHING. Reflect on and identify your core values as a teacher. Prioritize these principles. Write these principles down to share with your Circle of Friends. Discuss the origins of these principles and how they influence your teaching.

exercise

Weekly Reflections

On a scale of 1–10, gauge (a) **how effective you were as a teacher this week, and** (b) **how you are feeling this week**. What adjective might best capture your teaching and your feelings this week?

THURSDAY 23

FRIDAY 24

REMINDERS · NOTES · WEEKEND HOMEWORK

plan ahead

- **How does next week relate to this week?**
- **What continues to confuse or frustrate your students?**
- **Think of your class as a story: What should happen next?**
- **Who can help you be more successful next week?**

PERSONAL

WEEKLY FOCUS:

WEEKLY GOAL:

PROFESSIONAL

WEEKLY FOCUS:

WEEKLY GOAL:

Honor Your Roles

TIPS FOR *Teachers*

Learn to say "no." You do not have to do everything; in fact, you cannot. This is especially true if you have kids of your own or are part of a relationship with another person. Saying "no" to a committee or an "opportunity" means you are saying "yes" to some other person, event, or experience. Remember what is important and use that to help you choose the right path.

TIPS FOR *Teaching*

Be a model learner. Get to know your students so you can recommend books, strategies, or topics. Talk whenever appropriate about your own learning and interests; show them that you practice what you preach. Talk about when, why, where, how, and what you learn. Talk to students about how you choose strategies and books. Always model for them any assignments you give, so they hear how you approach a problem or a text.

MONDAY 27

TUESDAY 28

WEDNESDAY 29

The Teacher's Daybook by Jim Burke (Heinemann: Portsmouth, NH); © 2012 by Jim Burke.

celebrate

WATCH YOUR ENERGY. Keep a record of *everything* you do this week at home and at school. As you jot down an activity (e.g., grading papers, cooking dinner, going for a walk), indicate whether it Takes Energy (T), Gives Energy (G), or is Neutral (N), which means it does neither. After seven days, go back and examine the week's data. Bring your results to the next Circle of Friends get-together. What do you notice? What gives you energy? What takes it? What could you change to improve your energy? Read Don Graves' book *The Energy to Teach* (2001) for more ideas.

Weekly Reflections

On a scale of 1–10, gauge (a) *how effective you were as a teacher this week, and* (b) *how you are feeling this week*. What adjective might best capture your teaching and your feelings this week?

THURSDAY 30

FRIDAY 31

REMINDERS · NOTES · WEEKEND HOMEWORK

plan ahead

- How does next week relate to this week?
- What continues to confuse or frustrate your students?
- Think of your class as a story: What should happen next?
- Who can help you be more successful next week?

PERSONAL

WEEKLY FOCUS:

WEEKLY GOAL:

PROFESSIONAL

WEEKLY FOCUS:

WEEKLY GOAL:

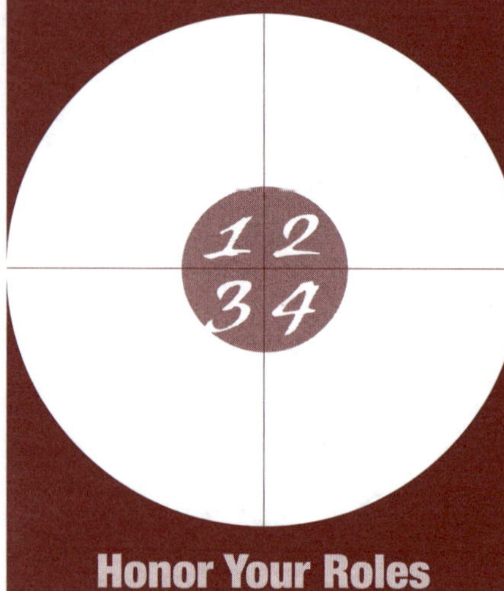

Honor Your Roles

TIPS FOR *Teachers*

Clip it! Put an extra paper clip (big one) on each period's roll sheet. Here you should clip all late slips, student summons notes, announcements, and admit slips. Students bombard you as they come in, giving you this note, that slip, all while you are trying to teach. Just collect them all, clip them to the page in your roll book, and get class started. Once they are down to work and you can take attendance, you can sort through the papers.

TIPS FOR *Teaching*

Use Literature Circles. There are four key roles that elicit insightful contributions from students: The **Discussion Director** creates good discussion questions, convenes the meeting, and solicits contributions from the other members. The **Illluminator** directs group members to crucial sections of the text and reads these passages aloud. The **Connector** helps the group make connections between the text and the real world. The **Illustrator** offers visual responses and explanations of the written text.

MONDAY 3

TUESDAY 4

WEDNESDAY 5

TIPS FOR *Professional Learning*

REVIEW SESSION. What's going well? What's not working? Revisit last week's data and discoveries about your energy. What changes can or did you make this week? Who could help you? What could they do for you?

Weekly Reflections

On a scale of 1–10, gauge (a) **how effective you were as a teacher this week, and** (b) **how you are feeling this week**. What adjective might best capture your teaching and your feelings this week?

THURSDAY 6

FRIDAY 7

REMINDERS · NOTES · WEEKEND HOMEWORK

plan ahead

▶ How does next week relate to this week?

▶ What continues to confuse or frustrate your students?

▶ Think of your class as a story: What should happen next?

▶ Who can help you be more successful next week?

PERSONAL

WEEKLY FOCUS:

WEEKLY GOAL:

PROFESSIONAL

WEEKLY FOCUS:

WEEKLY GOAL:

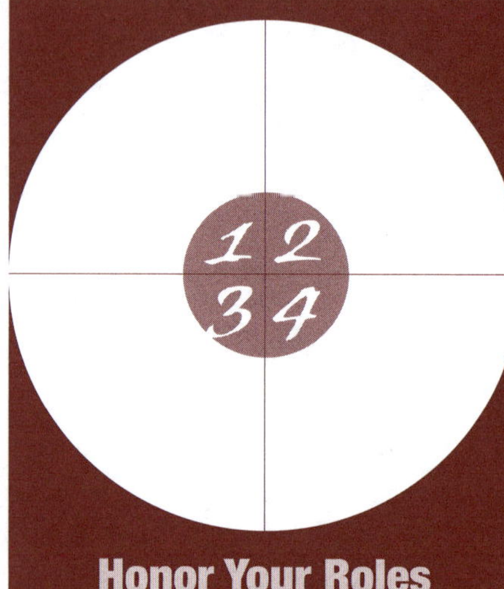

Honor Your Roles

TIPS FOR *Teachers*

Take home only what you can (and should!) do in one night. The eighty papers you just collected need to be read and graded, but not all in one night. Take home twenty, even twenty-five, and use the rest of your night to take care of yourself so you can be an effective teacher tomorrow.

TIPS FOR *Teaching*

Make room for essential conversations. Each discipline has at its heart certain vital questions its practitioners have spent decades, even centuries, trying to answer. When we make room for the essential conversations in our disciplines and invite students to enter into those discussions, we create opportunities for deep learning and thoughtful reading.

MONDAY 10

TUESDAY 11

WEDNESDAY 12

TIPS FOR *Professional Learning*

STEALING TIME. Take a magazine or book wherever you go (e.g., bank, movies, laundromat, dentist); if you have to wait, use the time to read. You might also keep some stationery, cards, or a journal with you in case you feel like writing instead. Ask others, especially those in your Circle of Friends, how they save time and work more efficiently.

Weekly Reflections

On a scale of 1–10, gauge (a) **how effective you were as a teacher this week, and** (b) **how you are feeling this week**. What adjective might best capture your teaching and your feelings this week?

THURSDAY 13

FRIDAY 14

REMINDERS · NOTES · WEEKEND HOMEWORK

plan ahead

➤ How does next week relate to this week?

➤ What continues to confuse or frustrate your students?

➤ Think of your class as a story: What should happen next?

➤ Who can help you be more successful next week?

PERSONAL

WEEKLY FOCUS:

WEEKLY GOAL:

PROFESSIONAL

WEEKLY FOCUS:

WEEKLY GOAL:

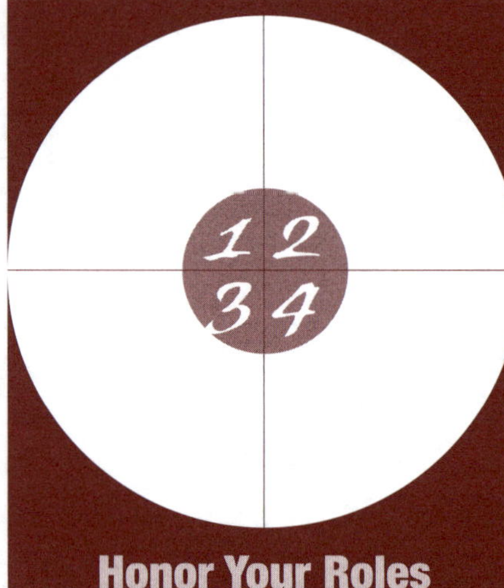

Honor Your Roles

TIPS FOR *Teachers*

Arrange your computer for efficiency. Create one folder for the school year (e.g., School 2011–12). Within that folder, create others such as: Freshman English, First Period, School Correspondence, Grades, Common Documents. Give all saved documents names you can easily search for: Giver_RResponse Sample, MathA_Ch1 Test. Avoid duplicating file names; you will end up with multiple editions of the same handouts.

TIPS FOR *Teaching*

Talk about learning. Using talk for different purposes in different contexts allows students the important opportunity they need to figure out what they think, in part by hearing what others think, after which they may revise their own thinking. Talking also helps students whose verbal skills need practice and development. ESL students need to hear how English is used and practice it for themselves in authentic academic contexts.

MONDAY 17

TUESDAY 18

WEDNESDAY 19

breathe

TIPS FOR *Professional Learning*

TAKE CARE. Identify and make an effort to spend time with those colleagues and students who:

- Make you laugh
- Give you ideas
- Give you strength
- Mentor you
- Nourish you
- Engage you

Obviously members of your Circle of Friends help to meet many of these needs. Now might be a good time to invite others around school to join your Circle.

Weekly Reflections

On a scale of 1–10, gauge (a) *how effective you were as a teacher this week, and* (b) *how you are feeling this week*. What adjective might best capture your teaching and your feelings this week?

THURSDAY 20

FRIDAY 21

REMINDERS · NOTES · WEEKEND HOMEWORK

plan ahead

- How does next week relate to this week?
- What continues to confuse or frustrate your students?
- Think of your class as a story: What should happen next?
- Who can help you be more successful next week?

PERSONAL

WEEKLY FOCUS:

WEEKLY GOAL:

PROFESSIONAL

WEEKLY FOCUS:

WEEKLY GOAL:

Honor Your Roles

TIPS FOR *Teachers*

Use your Master Binder. Each day's lesson plan should be hole punched, along with a copy of all notes, handouts, and overheads. These should be placed in the Master Binder in their appropriate sections. When the lesson is over, write notes on the lesson plan (or on the back) so if you teach it again, you can improve it. Also, add copies of useful student examples of this assignment when you collect them; it will help students in the future to see a sample of what you want.

TIPS FOR *Teaching*

Make connections. Connecting—ideas, authors, subjects—is what good thinkers do; it's one of the most satisfying experiences of thinking, in fact. It's that *Ah-ha!* moment. We need to connect what we have taught and will eventually teach so students recognize these links and experience our discipline as a coherent field of study. But students need to make other connections also: between themselves and the world outside, one subject and another, the past and the present, the personal and the public.

MONDAY 24

TUESDAY 25

WEDNESDAY 26

The Teacher's Daybook by Jim Burke (Heinemann: Portsmouth, NH); © 2012 by Jim Burke.

TIPS FOR *Professional Learning*

CHECK UP/CHECK IN. On a scale of 1–10, how are you feeling at this point? If you are a 10 (i.e., strong, engaged, healthy, happy), figure out why. Likewise, if you are a 1 (i.e., depressed, exhausted, disengaged), identify the causes and seek to address them (perhaps by revisiting some of the activities listed elsewhere in the *Daybook*). Share your scores with your Circle of Friends. Brainstorm solutions and offer support to those who are struggling.

confront

Weekly Reflections

On a scale of 1–10, gauge (a) **how effective you were as a teacher this week, and** (b) **how you are feeling this week**. What adjective might best capture your teaching and your feelings this week?

THURSDAY 27

FRIDAY 28

REMINDERS · NOTES · WEEKEND HOMEWORK

plan ahead

➤ How does next week relate to this week?

➤ What continues to confuse or frustrate your students?

➤ Think of your class as a story: What should happen next?

➤ Who can help you be more successful next week?

PERSONAL

WEEKLY FOCUS:

WEEKLY GOAL:

PROFESSIONAL

WEEKLY FOCUS:

WEEKLY GOAL:

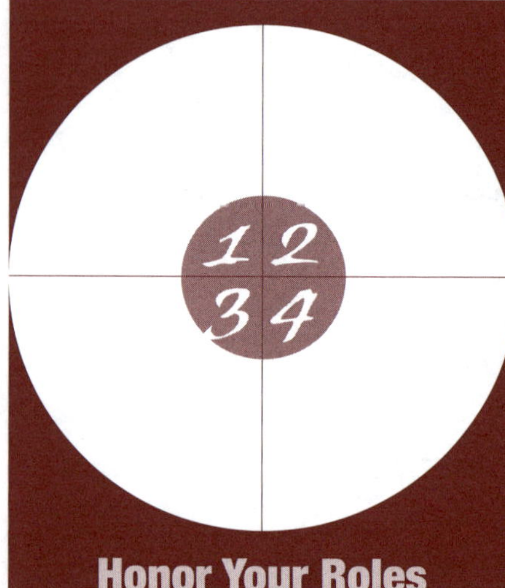

Honor Your Roles

TIPS FOR *Teachers*

Remember the dinner table test. To the old adage "Do no harm," add a new one: "Do nothing that will make parents say, 'Your teacher did/said what?!' when they ask, 'What did you do today in class?' at the dinner table."

TIPS FOR *Teaching*

Choose texts wisely. Ask the following questions to help you choose the texts you use: What will students need to know and be able to do to read this piece? How does it relate to what they read before and will read in the near future? Is this passage of genuine interest to the students? Will this text and the ideas within it inspire good conversation and engaged learning? Is it clear to the students why you are having them read this? Does it challenge *all* your students while being accessible enough for all your students to read it?

MONDAY 1

TUESDAY 2

WEDNESDAY 3

change

TIPS FOR *Professional Learning*

PERSONAL LEARNING. What are you doing to support your own learning? Plants that get no water dry up and die. You must water your own roots. Discuss your learning and strategies for doing so with members of your Circle. Consider doing one or more of the following:

- Read a professional journal.
- Buy a book you can read for fifteen minutes a day to learn something new.
- Keep a journal in which you write about your own teaching or subject matter.
- Always have something you are trying to learn to do better in the classroom or in your own life. Make it reasonable but meaningful.

Weekly Reflections

On a scale of 1–10, gauge (a) *how effective you were as a teacher this week, and* (b) *how you are feeling this week*. What adjective might best capture your teaching and your feelings this week?

THURSDAY 4

FRIDAY 5

REMINDERS · NOTES · WEEKEND HOMEWORK

plan ahead

- How does next week relate to this week?
- What continues to confuse or frustrate your students?
- Think of your class as a story: What should happen next?
- Who can help you be more successful next week?

PERSONAL

WEEKLY FOCUS:

WEEKLY GOAL:

PROFESSIONAL

WEEKLY FOCUS:

WEEKLY GOAL:

Honor Your Roles

TIPS FOR *Teachers*

Invest in your comfort and health. Your work demands long bouts of sitting and lots of writing and carrying. You have tools that you use every day; it makes sense to buy those tools that will make your work easier and take less of a toll on your body. For example, use ergonomically engineered chairs and keyboards. Writer Annie Lamott says the secret to good writing is having a comfortable chair. You can't enjoy your work or do it well if you are thinking about how much your hands ache or your butt hurts.

TIPS FOR *Teaching*

Provide options for student response. Because students read for a variety of purposes and in different ways, they need a range of options when they respond to their reading. Such choices allow for increased engagement and improved comprehension. Finally, allowing students to choose—writing, speaking, drawing—invites them to think about their learning in different ways and take more responsibility.

MONDAY 8

TUESDAY 9

WEDNESDAY 10

TIPS FOR *Professional Learning*

CELEBRATIONS. You've been working hard now for a couple of months. Do something to celebrate your own successes and hard work—in the classroom, around the school, and at home. Spend time with friends, go out to dinner with your Circle of Friends (and don't talk about work!), or take a day off to be with yourself, doing the things you need to do so you can return and continue to enjoy your work and the kids.

Weekly Reflections

On a scale of 1–10, gauge (a) **how effective you were as a teacher this week, and** (b) **how you are feeling this week**. What adjective might best capture your teaching and your feelings this week?

THURSDAY 11

FRIDAY 12

REMINDERS · NOTES · WEEKEND HOMEWORK

plan ahead

- How does next week relate to this week?
- What continues to confuse or frustrate your students?
- Think of your class as a story: What should happen next?
- Who can help you be more successful next week?

PERSONAL

WEEKLY FOCUS:

WEEKLY GOAL:

PROFESSIONAL

WEEKLY FOCUS:

WEEKLY GOAL:

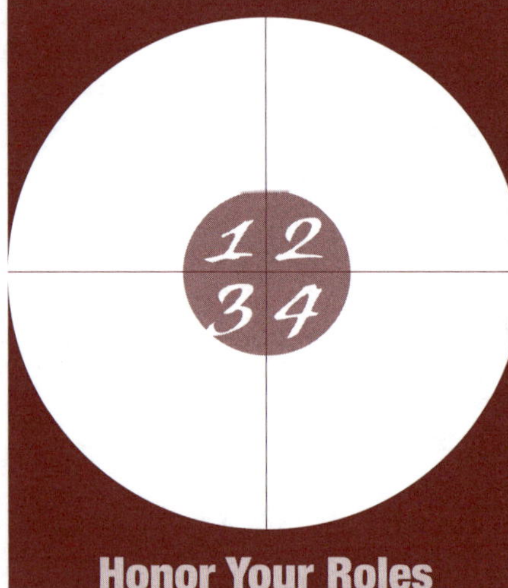

Honor Your Roles

TIPS FOR *Teachers*

Maximize time. Check the monthly calendar regularly to remind yourself of what is coming up. This vigilance will protect you from losing time when testing comes. Periodically reconcile the master calendar and your *Daybook* to keep your information current and avoid losing time to unforeseen events such as a two-hour emergency drill.

TIPS FOR *Teaching*

Develop guidelines for group discussions. Good class discussions are no accident: people must learn how to discuss ideas and texts. Discussions, whether in small groups or with the full class, offer students social occasions for learning and demonstrating their own learning to others.

MONDAY 15

TUESDAY 16

WEDNESDAY 17

TIPS FOR *Professional Learning*

THE STUDENT FROM HELL. Everyone has them, though they may change over the course of the year. So often, however, their difficulties spring from a more private, personal place that, if we can take time to understand, we will be able to address, thus becoming their most important teacher. Pick students from the past whose difficulties you came to understand; remind yourself that people can change. Now pick students from this year and list what they do, why (you think) they do it, and what you think will help you and your students be able to learn from each other. Share your stories and possible strategies—and laughter—with your Circle.

give

Weekly Reflections

On a scale of 1–10, gauge (a) **how effective you were as a teacher this week, and** (b) **how you are feeling this week**. What adjective might best capture your teaching and your feelings this week?

THURSDAY 18

FRIDAY 19

REMINDERS · NOTES · WEEKEND HOMEWORK

plan ahead

How does next week relate to this week?

What continues to confuse or frustrate your students?

Think of your class as a story: What should happen next?

Who can help you be more successful next week?

PERSONAL

WEEKLY FOCUS:

WEEKLY GOAL:

PROFESSIONAL

WEEKLY FOCUS:

WEEKLY GOAL:

Honor Your Roles

TIPS FOR *Teachers*

Plan ahead. If you are being evaluated, set up a portfolio of assignments and student examples from those assignments. Use the Professional Portfolio Page in the Appendices (p. 158) to keep track of all you do this year. Identify your professional or instructional goals up front, then ask daily, "Did I do anything I can/should add to my portfolio?"

TIPS FOR *Teaching*

Use video to support, not *replace* reading. Use video clips to help students *see* what they are reading about or studying. These clips should be cued up to help students quickly focus on that part of the video text that will help them prepare to read or better understand what they just read by improving their capacity to see what they read. Ask yourself when you consider using a video if its use in that instance is helping them not read. Interrupt to discuss and take notes to get best results.

MONDAY 22

TUESDAY 23

WEDNESDAY 24

join

BE A MENTOR. Think about the new or struggling teachers you know. What can you do to give them a boost, help them along, or just keep them going strong? Consider sharing a lesson, recommending a book, eating lunch with them, or even inviting them to join your Circle of Friends. Of course you may have one or two students you want to mentor. You have so much to offer them; go for it!

Weekly Reflections

On a scale of 1–10, gauge (a) *how effective you were as a teacher this week,* and (b) *how you are feeling this week.* What adjective might best capture your teaching and your feelings this week?

THURSDAY 25

FRIDAY 26

REMINDERS · NOTES · WEEKEND HOMEWORK

plan ahead

- How does next week relate to this week?
- What continues to confuse or frustrate your students?
- Think of your class as a story: What should happen next?
- Who can help you be more successful next week?

PERSONAL

WEEKLY FOCUS:

WEEKLY GOAL:

PROFESSIONAL

WEEKLY FOCUS:

WEEKLY GOAL:

Honor Your Roles

TIPS FOR *Teachers*

Know the rules and protocols. Each school and district has its own culture and rules. These change annually in some cases. All teachers, but especially new teachers, need to learn what is expected. Find someone to be your resource person in this area. Specific areas for which to inquire about the rules: films, photocopying, school events, open house, anything to do with money, visitors to your classroom, field trips, and use of materials.

TIPS FOR *Teaching*

Use various strategies. Effective learners not only have an array of strategies to choose from but know when and how to use them. The strategies that help one student better understand his history textbook do not necessarily help the girl or the ESL student. Thus we must use and help students master a range of strategies, discussing as part of that process when, why, and how to use each one. Students, by reflecting on their own learning, will eventually identify those that help them the most.

MONDAY 29

TUESDAY 30

WEDNESDAY 31

TIPS FOR *Professional Learning*

trust

READ AND REFLECT ON YOUR FIELD OF STUDY. Time to begin thinking about the year ahead. Find a book or three, or some professional journals you saved from last year. Think about some area of teaching—reading, writing, thinking, speaking—you want to improve on this year; choose some readings that can help you begin to act on that plan.

Weekly Reflections

On a scale of 1–10, gauge (a) *how effective you were as a teacher this week, and* (b) *how you are feeling this week*. What adjective might best capture your teaching and your feelings this week?

THURSDAY 1

FRIDAY 2

REMINDERS · NOTES · WEEKEND HOMEWORK

plan ahead

➤ How does next week relate to this week?

➤ What continues to confuse or frustrate your students?

➤ Think of your class as a story: What should happen next?

➤ Who can help you be more successful next week?

PERSONAL

WEEKLY FOCUS:

WEEKLY GOAL:

PROFESSIONAL

WEEKLY FOCUS:

WEEKLY GOAL:

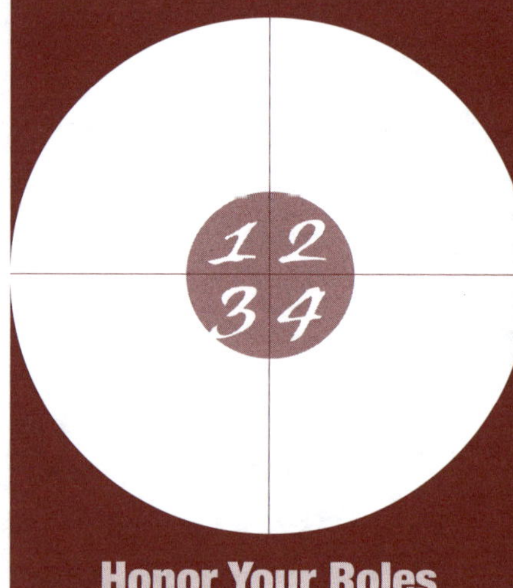

Honor Your Roles

TIPS FOR *Teachers*

Keep track. Use the various information tools included in your *Daybook* to record important information. Keep your substitute record up to date (on the Teacher's Homepage). Also keep your eyes open for days you can take off without any consequence for your students. Monitor your Professional Portfolio Page for delinquent reimbursements.

TIPS FOR *Teaching*

Use questions to support learning. Your first question, once you have established the foundational information—who, where, why, when, what, how—should be "What are the questions we need to ask about this subject (or text)?" This changes your role from poser to facilitator as you solicit questions and decide which ones to consider. Practice developing good questions and learn to establish criteria for good questions.

MONDAY 5

TUESDAY 6

WEDNESDAY 7

learn

TIPS FOR *Professional Learning*

FIRST-DRAFT TEACHING. Writer Annie Lamott, in her book *Bird by Bird* (1994), talks about giving yourself permission to write "shitty first drafts" when you are beginning a new piece of writing. List out those things—texts, techniques, or ideas—you are doing for the first time this year. Give yourself permission to do them badly and learn from those mistakes so you will do them better next time. Share what you are doing and how it's going with your Circle; see if they have any suggestions that will help you.

Weekly Reflections

On a scale of 1–10, gauge (a) *how effective you were as a teacher this week,* and (b) *how you are feeling this week*. What adjective might best capture your teaching and your feelings this week?

THURSDAY 8

FRIDAY 9

REMINDERS · NOTES · WEEKEND HOMEWORK

plan ahead

- How does next week relate to this week?
- What continues to confuse or frustrate your students?
- Think of your class as a story: What should happen next?
- Who can help you be more successful next week?

PERSONAL

WEEKLY FOCUS:

WEEKLY GOAL:

PROFESSIONAL

WEEKLY FOCUS:

WEEKLY GOAL:

Honor Your Roles

TIPS FOR *Teachers*

Save money. If you do your work at home, take home the supplies you need to do that work. Supplies such as sticky notes, correction fluid, rubber bands, paper clips, pens, and even paper all add up quickly when you work as hard as you do. Don't pay to work; let the school pay your way so you can use that money for yourself or your own kids.

TIPS FOR *Teaching*

Prepare students to learn. Familiarize students with ideas and content; activate their prior knowledge; establish a purpose; clarify how they should read a particular text; allow them to evaluate their needs and the demands of the assignment; help them create a mental outline in their heads so information can be effectively organized as they read it; show them how to identify potential problems.

MONDAY 12

TUESDAY 13

WEDNESDAY 14

TIPS FOR *Professional Learning*

eat (well)

PRACTICAL REFLECTIONS. In *The Teacher Book*, Bobbi Fisher (2000) offers two activities to help teachers stay engaged and healthy. She asks people to choose a specific domain (e.g., writing) and use the following prompts to help them understand what they need and can do to improve in that area:

- I get stressed when . . .
- Currently I . . .
- I would like to do less . . .
- It helps when . . .
- I would like to . . .
- I would like to do more . . .

Use these prompts to guide the discussion with your Circle of Friends. Consider writing about them before you meet with your Circle.

Weekly Reflections

On a scale of 1–10, gauge (a) *how effective you were as a teacher this week, and* (b) *how you are feeling this week*. What adjective might best capture your teaching and your feelings this week?

THURSDAY 15

FRIDAY 16

REMINDERS · NOTES · WEEKEND HOMEWORK

plan ahead

- How does next week relate to this week?
- What continues to confuse or frustrate your students?
- Think of your class as a story: What should happen next?
- Who can help you be more successful next week?

PERSONAL

WEEKLY FOCUS:

WEEKLY GOAL:

PROFESSIONAL

WEEKLY FOCUS:

WEEKLY GOAL:

Honor Your Roles

TIPS FOR *Teachers*

Make it easy for the sub—and yourself.
Preparing for a sub is a hassle. Make a photocopy of the Substitute Information Template in the Appendix. Fill this in and gather the different documents mentioned on it. Use your computer to write up a lesson plan template for substitutes; then fax it to school with a note saying where the Substitute Information packet is located.

TIPS FOR *Teaching*

Teach vocabulary strategies. Janet Allen (1995) says: "Look at the word in relation to the sentence. Look the word up in the dictionary and see if any meanings fit the sentence. Ask the teacher [or someone else who might know]. Sound it out. Read the sentence again. Look at the beginning of the sentence again. Look for other key words in the sentence that might tell you the meaning. Think what makes sense. Ask a friend to read the sentence. Read around the word and then go back again. Look at the picture if there is one. Skip it if you don't need to know it."

MONDAY 19

TUESDAY 20

WEDNESDAY 21

TIPS FOR *Professional Learning*

wait

REACH OUT. Consider contacting the parents of one or three kids who don't usually hear from teachers. Tell them something the student did better or even well. If you don't feel like calling, take five minutes to email as many notes to these same kids or their parents, telling them you appreciate their recent effort and you see the difference it makes. Brainstorm other ways of reaching out with your Circle. Don't forget to reach out—through winks, notes, and offers—to your colleagues.

Weekly Reflections

On a scale of 1–10, gauge (a) *how effective you were as a teacher this week, and* (b) *how you are feeling this week*. What adjective might best capture your teaching and your feelings this week?

THURSDAY 22

FRIDAY 23

REMINDERS · NOTES · WEEKEND HOMEWORK

plan ahead

➤ How does next week relate to this week?

➤ What continues to confuse or frustrate your students?

➤ Think of your class as a story: What should happen next?

➤ Who can help you be more successful next week?

PERSONAL

WEEKLY FOCUS:

WEEKLY GOAL:

PROFESSIONAL

WEEKLY FOCUS:

WEEKLY GOAL:

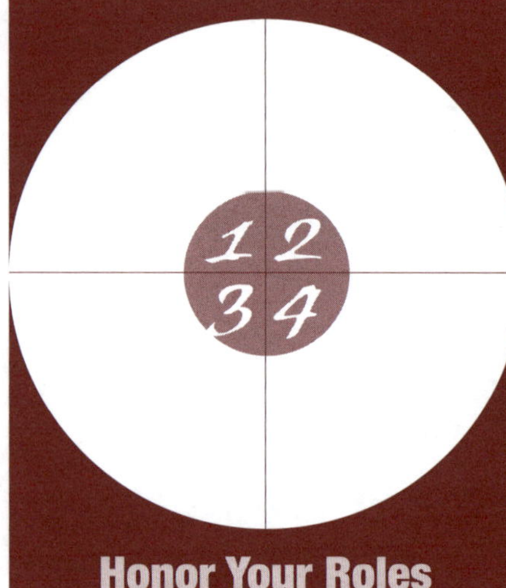

Honor Your Roles

TIPS FOR *Teachers*

Keep a "bug list." This is a list of things that bug you about your classroom, your equipment, whatever; you must be able to do something about it, however. Show it to a colleague or administrator and ask them how to solve some of these nagging problems. Offer the same advice to a colleague who asks for your assistance.

TIPS FOR *Teaching*

Use graphic organizers. Use graphic organizers to develop students' skills and strategies. Discuss why you chose the ones you did. Gradually allow students to choose the method that works best for them. Ask students why they made the choices they did so they can be more aware of their thought processes when making such decisions as which tool or technique to use when thinking about a specific assignment.

MONDAY 26

TUESDAY 27

WEDNESDAY 28

mentor

TIPS FOR *Professional Learning*

ROUNDTABLE OF INFLUENCE. So often our identity as teachers originates in some teacher we had along the way. List your most important role models or influences. Whether they were teachers or not, list the qualities that inspired you or the lessons they taught you. Reflect on how they achieved these qualities or taught these lessons. Trade stories with your Circle of Friends.

Weekly Reflections

On a scale of 1–10, gauge (a) *how effective you were as a teacher this week, and* (b) *how you are feeling this week*. What adjective might best capture your teaching and your feelings this week?

THURSDAY 29

FRIDAY 30

REMINDERS · NOTES · WEEKEND HOMEWORK

plan ahead

➤ How does next week relate to this week?

➤ What continues to confuse or frustrate your students?

➤ Think of your class as a story: What should happen next?

➤ Who can help you be more successful next week?

PERSONAL

WEEKLY FOCUS:

WEEKLY GOAL:

PROFESSIONAL

WEEKLY FOCUS:

WEEKLY GOAL:

Honor Your Roles

TIPS FOR *Teachers*

Maximize your time. Always bring something you can do while waiting. Whether it's the copy machine or the bank, a meeting or a visit to the counselor's office—anywhere you might have to wait a few minutes—you will feel productive and relaxed because you have something to do. Of course you can bring papers to grade, but something like the *New Yorker* is more fun and stimulating and very discrete.

TIPS FOR *Teaching*

Teach students how to ask for help. Model for students in different circumstances how they might ask for help. I will say, when discussing a certain text, "I often get confused by ______. So when I come across such trouble, I ask someone else how they read that passage." As you develop such questions, put the best ones (e.g., "What is the author ______ing . . . ?") on a whiteboard or a poster.

MONDAY 3

TUESDAY 4

WEDNESDAY 5

delegate

GET AWAY. The *Tao Te Ching* says that we must do our work and step away from it. It's time you got away from work to renew yourself and your ties to those people and activities you love. Don't bring work home this week. You have a right to a life outside of school. Choose a good book to read or surround yourself with friends, films, or foods that nourish you. Write a note to the members of your Circle reminding them to take a break, too—or take one together!

Weekly Reflections

On a scale of 1–10, gauge (a) **how effective you were as a teacher this week, and** (b) **how you are feeling this week**. What adjective might best capture your teaching and your feelings this week?

THURSDAY 6

FRIDAY 7

REMINDERS · NOTES · WEEKEND HOMEWORK

plan ahead

▸ How does next week relate to this week?

▸ What continues to confuse or frustrate your students?

▸ Think of your class as a story: What should happen next?

▸ Who can help you be more successful next week?

PERSONAL

WEEKLY FOCUS:

WEEKLY GOAL:

PROFESSIONAL

WEEKLY FOCUS:

WEEKLY GOAL:

Honor Your Roles

TIPS FOR *Teachers*

Don't carry more than you must. Bring an extra copy of any class textbooks home so you don't have to always drag that monster around. Don't bring home eighty papers when all you will—and should—read that night are twenty-five. Don't lug three pounds worth of scissors, markers, and other supplies wherever you go; create a kit with those things and keep it in a secure place, only carrying it when you really must.

TIPS FOR *Teaching*

Provide good directions. In order to learn, students must understand the assignment. Directions—written, spoken, explained, or created—are complicated or helpful to the degree that they are clear and consider the students' needs. A single word in a sentence—*define* instead of *describe*—can make a crucial difference in one's performance on the task.

MONDAY 10

TUESDAY 11

WEDNESDAY 12

The Teacher's Daybook by Jim Burke (Heinemann: Portsmouth, NH); © 2012 by Jim Burke.

TIPS FOR *Professional Learning*

REVISIT GOALS. Enough time has passed that you should have made progress toward your personal and professional goals. Take yourself out to a café after work and review your goals worksheets. Ask yourself what you have done to achieve them; think about what has and has not worked. Identify what will help you make more progress so you achieve these goals by year's end. Or, revise the goals as needed in light of any changes that may have occurred since you originally set these goals. Brainstorm possible solutions with members of your Circle if you are not making progress in one area.

simplify

Weekly Reflections

On a scale of 1–10, gauge (a) *how effective you were as a teacher this week, and* (b) *how you are feeling this week*. What adjective might best capture your teaching and your feelings this week?

THURSDAY 13

FRIDAY 14

REMINDERS · NOTES · WEEKEND HOMEWORK

plan ahead

- How does next week relate to this week?
- What continues to confuse or frustrate your students?
- Think of your class as a story: What should happen next?
- Who can help you be more successful next week?

PERSONAL

WEEKLY FOCUS:

WEEKLY GOAL:

PROFESSIONAL

WEEKLY FOCUS:

WEEKLY GOAL:

Honor Your Roles

TIPS FOR *Teachers*

Maintain key relationships. Do what you must to get to know the plant manager and custodial staff. Know and maintain your relationship with the person who handles finances at school. Know the principal's secretary. Be sure the person who handles textbooks and school supplies knows and likes you. You will ask these people for help all year long; they are your essential resources. You can never thank them enough.

TIPS FOR *Teaching*

Go Fish! Lundin, Paul, and Christensen (2000) identify four key principles to improve morale and performance. (1) Choose your attitude. (2) Play. (3) Make their day. (4) Be present. These techniques came from Lundin's observations of the Pike Place Fish Market in Seattle, a world-famous market where they hurl the fish around and involve the customers in the experience. Think about how you can apply these four concepts to your work as a teacher. Note also that *play* is central to both Lundin's and Beckman's principles of effective teaching and learning.

MONDAY 17

TUESDAY 18

WEDNESDAY 19

TIPS FOR *Professional Learning*

encourage

REVIEW. RENEW. RETURN. Review your notes and activities from the first month last year. Renew your commitment to teaching and to kids. Return to school when there is some calm about the place, taking pleasure in the quiet hours in your room where you can begin to prepare for, to imagine, and to create the year ahead. Then dare to enjoy that year, leaning into the wind of each storm with the calm assurance that you know where you are going and, with your Circle of Friends, will be able to get there.

Weekly Reflections

On a scale of 1–10, gauge (a) *how effective you were as a teacher this week, and* (b) *how you are feeling this week*. What adjective might best capture your teaching and your feelings this week?

THURSDAY 20

FRIDAY 21

REMINDERS · NOTES · WEEKEND HOMEWORK

plan ahead

▶ How does next week relate to this week?

▶ What continues to confuse or frustrate your students?

▶ Think of your class as a story: What should happen next?

▶ Who can help you be more successful next week?

PERSONAL

WEEKLY FOCUS:

WEEKLY GOAL:

PROFESSIONAL

WEEKLY FOCUS:

WEEKLY GOAL:

Honor Your Roles

TIPS FOR *Teachers*

Read and weed. 1. Remove all contents from mailbox at school. 2. Stand directly in front of the box marked "Recycling." 3. Read each piece and choose one of three options: toss, read, not sure. 4. Do not move away from the box. 5. Go back through and decide: read or weed. 6. Walk away with only what you need. You've not only saved time but the environment, too.

TIPS FOR *Teaching*

Create and use study guides. Study guides (aka "tutors in print form") aid students *as they read*, not after. There are many types of guides, each helping students in a different way. Study guides provide useful structure for all students as they learn to think in new ways or encounter difficult texts on their way toward independence; they are especially helpful to learners with special needs and diverse abilities.

MONDAY 24

TUESDAY 25

WEDNESDAY 26

enjoy

TIPS FOR *Professional Learning*

CHALLENGE YOURSELF. If we are not challenged, we grow bored—everything becomes routine. The next stretch of the year provides a good opportunity to challenge yourself and your students. Take a risk; try something new or do something differently. Brainstorm ideas with your Circle that would give you all the chance to make a contribution to the school. Try to write a grant for a new program or improved tools to do your work. Bring some speakers in. Organize a field trip. Hold a writing or art contest.

Weekly Reflections

On a scale of 1–10, gauge (a) *how effective you were as a teacher this week, and* (b) *how you are feeling this week*. What adjective might best capture your teaching and your feelings this week?

THURSDAY 27

FRIDAY 28

REMINDERS · NOTES · WEEKEND HOMEWORK

plan ahead

- How does next week relate to this week?
- What continues to confuse or frustrate your students?
- Think of your class as a story: What should happen next?
- Who can help you be more successful next week?

Honor Your Roles

TIPS FOR *Teachers*

Take what you need from what you read. Don't carry around all those memos that tell you when a meeting is. Skim the memo; find the date, time, and location; jot this info into your *Daybook*; and recycle the memo. You're saving time, space, your back, and the environment.

TIPS FOR *Teaching*

Support students with special needs. Be multimodal, use multimedia—it helps all of your students, but the special ed students in particular. Whenever possible, let them hear it, talk about it, see it, and touch it. Sequence your activities and assignments logically. Provide a weekly assignment sheet to help them check off work they have done or need to do. Check frequently for understanding.

MONDAY 31

TUESDAY 1

WEDNESDAY 2

choose

TIPS FOR *Professional Learning*

TEACH AND REACH ALL STUDENTS. We all face challenges in our classes, many of which could prevent us from being a good teacher if we let them. What are you doing that works and what can you do to help the kids with special needs in your classes? If you do not know, find a colleague, a book, or an organization that can help you teach these students effectively. Pool your ideas and generate others with your Circle next time you meet. For more information, visit www.allkindsofminds.org.

Weekly Reflections

On a scale of 1–10, gauge (a) *how effective you were as a teacher this week, and* (b) *how you are feeling this week*. What adjective might best capture your teaching and your feelings this week?

THURSDAY 3

FRIDAY 4

REMINDERS · NOTES · WEEKEND HOMEWORK

plan ahead

▶ How does next week relate to this week?

▶ What continues to confuse or frustrate your students?

▶ Think of your class as a story: What should happen next?

▶ Who can help you be more successful next week?

PERSONAL

WEEKLY FOCUS:

WEEKLY GOAL:

PROFESSIONAL

WEEKLY FOCUS:

WEEKLY GOAL:

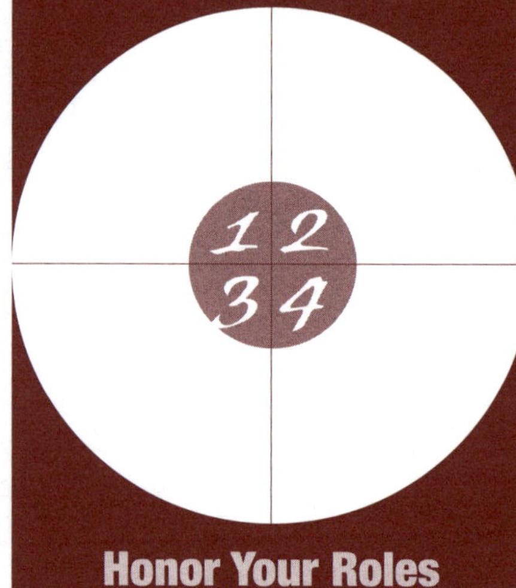

Honor Your Roles

TIPS FOR *Teachers*

A place for everything and everything in its place. Create sustainable, dedicated spaces to store everything from supplies to information. The Master Binder covers student information. The Professional Portfolio Page keeps track of your professional information. Dedicate a shelf for your editions of the books you teach. Consider a bulletin board for posting announcements and a class calendar. In and Out boxes are essential; however, having a place to put those papers once you take them out is also important and keeps you from losing papers.

TIPS FOR *Teaching*

Support English language learners. Assign the ESL student a language partner who is responsible for helping that student understand assignments and words they do not understand. Have a dictionary in their native language available. There are dictionaries that are specifically designed for English language learners. Have at least one of these in your class. Use gestures to emphasize and illustrate whenever possible.

MONDAY 7

TUESDAY 8

WEDNESDAY 9

TIPS FOR *Professional Learning*

TEACHING MINDS. Someone once said that children enter school as question marks and graduate as periods—a brutal statement but one that invites us to think about what we are accomplishing in our classes. What are you doing to make room for discovery, to challenge your students to think in different ways about different subjects? Share your ideas with your Circle; brainstorm new ways to engage and challenge your students.

create

Weekly Reflections

On a scale of 1–10, gauge (a) *how effective you were as a teacher this week,* and (b) *how you are feeling this week.* What adjective might best capture your teaching and your feelings this week?

THURSDAY 10

FRIDAY 11

REMINDERS · NOTES · WEEKEND HOMEWORK

plan ahead

- How does next week relate to this week?
- What continues to confuse or frustrate your students?
- Think of your class as a story: What should happen next?
- Who can help you be more successful next week?

PERSONAL

WEEKLY FOCUS:

WEEKLY GOAL:

PROFESSIONAL

WEEKLY FOCUS:

WEEKLY GOAL:

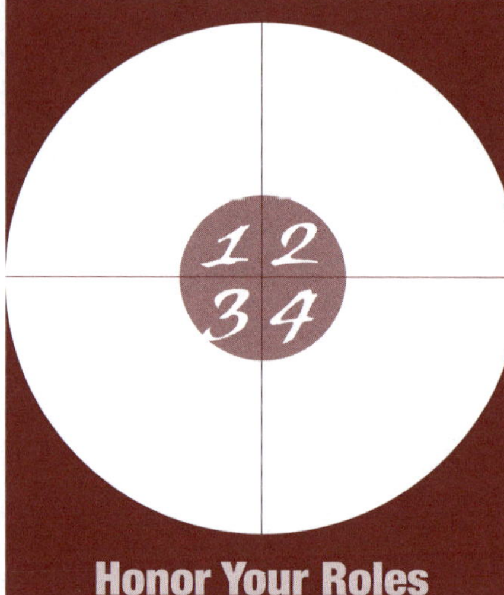

Honor Your Roles

TIPS FOR *Teachers*

Back up everything. This means mostly backing up your computer files, but also refers to hard copies. Put a sticky note on your original handout and write "Master" on it, so that when you copy it in the future you will always get the best quality. Keep all your teaching documents in one folder (e.g., "School Work") so you can quickly back up the whole folder.

TIPS FOR *Teaching*

Teach by design. Ask these design questions: What do I want the students to be able to do? Why do I want them to be able to do that? What activities will lead to this outcome? What examples can I provide to help students see what strong and weak performances look like on this assignment? What do they need to know or be able to do to accomplish that? What evidence of their performance/achievement is acceptable?

MONDAY 14

TUESDAY 15

WEDNESDAY 16

love

Professional Learning

YOUR PERSONAL AND PROFESSIONAL CANON. You no doubt have books that have influenced your personal and professional life. Make a list of those books that contributed the most to your ideas about life and teaching. Write a brief explanation of what each one taught you. Meet and discuss your list over lunch or a nice meal with your Circle of Friends.

Weekly Reflections

On a scale of 1–10, gauge (a) *how effective you were as a teacher this week, and* (b) *how you are feeling this week*. What adjective might best capture your teaching and your feelings this week?

THURSDAY 17

FRIDAY 18

REMINDERS · NOTES · WEEKEND HOMEWORK

plan ahead

▸ How does next week relate to this week?

▸ What continues to confuse or frustrate your students?

▸ Think of your class as a story: What should happen next?

▸ Who can help you be more successful next week?

WEEKLY FOCUS:

WEEKLY GOAL:

PROFESSIONAL

WEEKLY FOCUS:

WEEKLY GOAL:

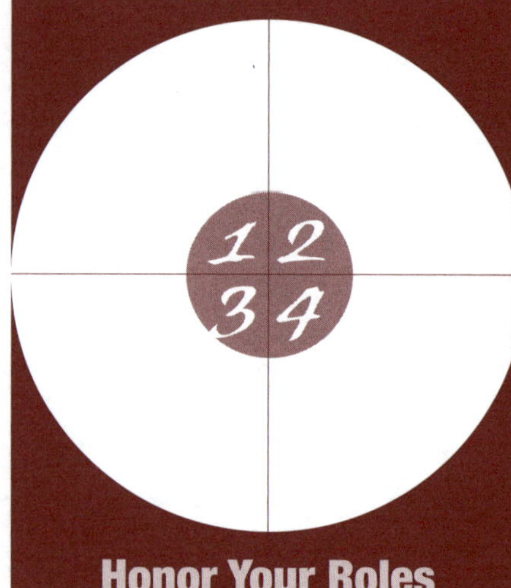

Honor Your Roles

TIPS FOR *Teachers*

Keep a stash. Don't hoard, but keep adequate supplies on hand. Hide a few extra xerographic transparencies in your box in the main office so you don't have to lose time walking back to your office to get some when you need them. If you need one whiteboard pen, take two so you don't have to interrupt your class next time. Tell the technology director you need an ink cartridge before you really do; then when it does run out, you won't lose valuable class time.

TIPS FOR *Teaching*

Teach and support students. Use different questioning strategies. Challenge and support students. Provide options for responding. Prepare them to read. Use video to support instruction. Use graphic organizers. Develop guidelines for discussion. Use questions to support. Teach vocabulary strategies. Teach students how to ask for help. Provide good directions. Create and use study guides. Support students with special needs. Make connections. Support students with learning difficulties. Support English language learners.

MONDAY 21

TUESDAY 22

WEDNESDAY 23

The Teacher's Daybook by Jim Burke (Heinemann: Portsmouth, NH); © 2012 by Jim Burke.

TIPS FOR *Professional Learning*

WHAT'S MISSING? We teach best what we know and like most. This means that we sometimes ignore or avoid other subjects. What are the skills or areas of the curriculum you are not getting to, and what can you do to address students' needs in those areas? If possible, find a colleague who can mentor you in that area, one who seems to have strength in that domain. Find out how members of your Circle address this tricky aspect of their work.

refuse

Weekly Reflections

On a scale of 1–10, gauge (a) **how effective you were as a teacher this week, and** (b) **how you are feeling this week**. What adjective might best capture your teaching and your feelings this week?

THURSDAY 24

FRIDAY 25

REMINDERS · NOTES · WEEKEND HOMEWORK

plan ahead

▸ How does next week relate to this week?

▸ What continues to confuse or frustrate your students?

▸ Think of your class as a story: What should happen next?

▸ Who can help you be more successful next week?

PERSONAL

WEEKLY FOCUS:

WEEKLY GOAL:

PROFESSIONAL

WEEKLY FOCUS:

WEEKLY GOAL:

Honor Your Roles

TIPS FOR *Teachers*

Create a toolkit. We use so many supplies for our work. Any time spent looking for them is time lost. Go to a good office or art supply store and find a bag or briefcase that meets your needs. Sometimes more specialized stores like luggage stores or online companies carry items specifically designed to meet different uses. Stock it with whatever you use at school and home—extra leads, colored pens, overhead pens, sticky notes, protractors, batteries, a cutter, a compass.

TIPS FOR *Teaching*

Check for understanding and growth. Both teacher and student must ask what they achieved when they finish an assignment. The only way to improve is to compare how you did with what you wanted or were expected to accomplish. Such information is only useful, however, to the degree that it improves future performances. Finally, understanding can only be assessed by multiple measures, all of which contribute to a more complete picture of the students and their performance.

MONDAY 28

TUESDAY 29

WEDNESDAY 30

TIPS FOR *Professional Learning*

MAKE ROOM FOR WHAT YOU LOVE. All teachers have some component of their subject area that is special to them. Bring that passion, those talents, into the classroom. It shows kids what you love about your subject; this helps them better understand why you want to teach it or how your subject applies to the world. Help them see in your subject what led you to want to teach it. Share your passion with your Circle and explain how you incorporate it into your teaching.

accept

Weekly Reflections

On a scale of 1–10, gauge (a) *how effective you were as a teacher this week*, and (b) *how you are feeling this week*. What adjective might best capture your teaching and your feelings this week?

THURSDAY 31

FRIDAY 1

REMINDERS · NOTES · WEEKEND HOMEWORK

plan ahead

➤ How does next week relate to this week?

➤ What continues to confuse or frustrate your students?

➤ Think of your class as a story: What should happen next?

➤ Who can help you be more successful next week?

PERSONAL

WEEKLY FOCUS:

WEEKLY GOAL:

PROFESSIONAL

WEEKLY FOCUS:

WEEKLY GOAL:

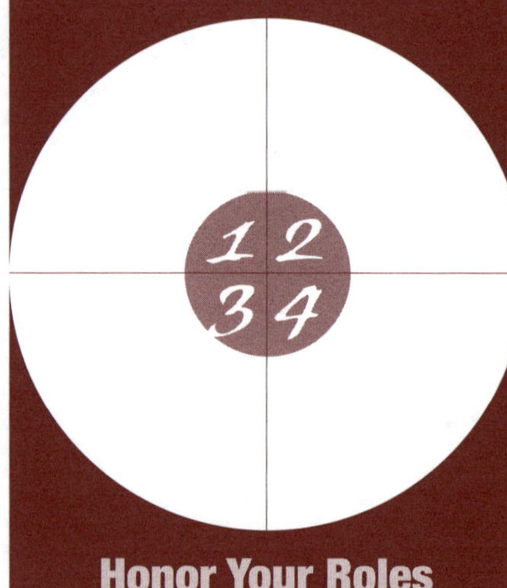

Honor Your Roles

TIPS FOR *Teachers*

To break up the tedium of grading, take short breaks and try the following: Visit interesting blogs like www.postsecret.com or indexed. blogspot.com; catch up on the latest news at www.nytimes.com or www.cnn.com; or watch 15 minutes of a great television show on a DVD you keep ready in your computer; stretch, exercise, or do yoga.

TIPS FOR *Teaching*

Look for ways to incorporate more technology and 21st-century literacies into your curriculum. Check out the Partnership for 21st Century Skills at www.21stcenturyskills.org, visit www.thinkfinity.org, or go to www. readwritethink.org.

MONDAY 4

TUESDAY 5

WEDNESDAY 6

hope

TIPS FOR *Professional Learning*

MAKE TIME TO READ! New books are coming out in all subject areas all the time. Most teachers have to travel to work, leaving them time each day to read books that can enrich us both personally and professionally. Consider listening to audiobooks. Go to audible.com and search for a book or subject that interests you and will allow you to make interesting connections in your class. I listen to about two books a month and find they inevitably improve my teaching by allowing me to make connections for myself and my students.

Weekly Reflections

On a scale of 1–10, gauge (a) *how effective you were as a teacher this week,* and (b) *how you are feeling this week*. What adjective might best capture your teaching and your feelings this week?

THURSDAY 7

FRIDAY 8

REMINDERS · NOTES · WEEKEND HOMEWORK

plan ahead

➤ How does next week relate to this week?

➤ What continues to confuse or frustrate your students?

➤ Think of your class as a story: What should happen next?

➤ Who can help you be more successful next week?

PERSONAL

WEEKLY FOCUS:

WEEKLY GOAL:

PROFESSIONAL

WEEKLY FOCUS:

WEEKLY GOAL:

Honor Your Roles

TIPS FOR *Teachers*

Plan ahead. Save time by thinking ahead about needed resources. Reserve the computer lab well in advance so you are sure you have it. Order supplies or resources you will need so they are there when you need them. Also, if your school demands that you sign up for resources and facilities and substitutes through the Internet, bookmark those sites for quick access.

TIPS FOR *Teaching*

Ask different types of questions. Asking and answering questions places the student in a more active role. They must create either meaningful questions or meaningful answers to these queries, then provide support for their thinking. Just as we use different types of tools for different jobs, so too must we use a variety of types of questions to help us think in different ways and at different levels about the subjects we study.

MONDAY 11

TUESDAY 12

WEDNESDAY 13

TIPS FOR *Professional Learning*

REVISIT YOUR PRINCIPLES. As testing season approaches it is important to remember what you value, what you are trying to accomplish as a teacher. How can you help your students succeed on the tests without sacrificing those principles that mean the most to you? Get together with your Circle to gain perspective on testing and gather strategies. Consider inviting some new teachers to your Circle on this occasion.

remember

Weekly Reflections

On a scale of 1–10, gauge (a) *how effective you were as a teacher this week, and* (b) *how you are feeling this week*. What adjective might best capture your teaching and your feelings this week?

THURSDAY 14

FRIDAY 15

REMINDERS · NOTES · WEEKEND HOMEWORK

plan ahead

- How does next week relate to this week?
- What continues to confuse or frustrate your students?
- Think of your class as a story: What should happen next?
- Who can help you be more successful next week?

PERSONAL

WEEKLY FOCUS:

WEEKLY GOAL:

PROFESSIONAL

WEEKLY FOCUS:

WEEKLY GOAL:

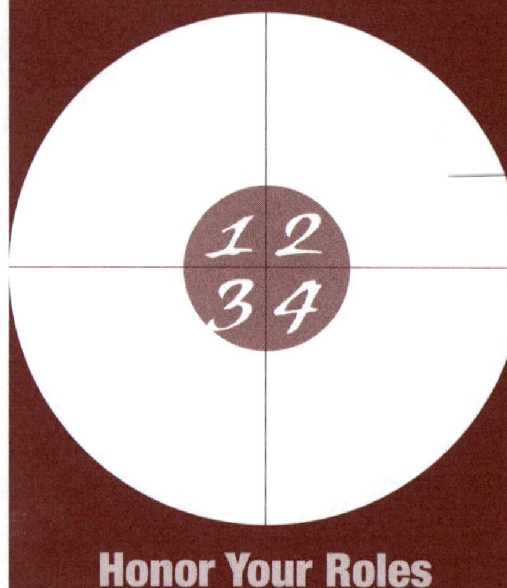

Honor Your Roles

TIPS FOR *Teachers*

Get free classroom materials. Most local newspapers make class sets available to teachers for free. Call the local paper to see what it offers; it is often called the Newspapers in Education (NIE) program. Get free samples—of books, posters, materials, and software—at professional conferences. Tell parents what you need through monthly letters home or letters to your school's parent group.

TIPS FOR *Teaching*

Use repeated reading. Repeated reading helps all readers read difficult texts. It is used in more controlled ways at the lower elementary grades, but from upper elementary through high school it provides useful support to readers who find themselves challenged by the demands of a particular text. The strategy not only increases comprehension but raises readers' confidence and engagement.

MONDAY 18

TUESDAY 19

WEDNESDAY 20

TIPS FOR *Professional Learning*

EXPAND THE CONVERSATION. Sometimes we are so hurried we do not have the conversations—with our colleagues, our religious mentors, our family, or even ourselves—that we need. Make time this week to schedule such conversations. If you "just don't have the time," consider reaching out through email to colleagues or friends. Now might be a good time to invite a couple of new people to join your Circle of Friends, or join an online community like www.englishcompanion.ning.com.

praise

Weekly Reflections

On a scale of 1–10, gauge (a) *how effective you were as a teacher this week, and* (b) *how you are feeling this week*. What adjective might best capture your teaching and your feelings this week?

THURSDAY 21

FRIDAY 22

REMINDERS · NOTES · WEEKEND HOMEWORK

plan ahead

- How does next week relate to this week?
- What continues to confuse or frustrate your students?
- Think of your class as a story: What should happen next?
- Who can help you be more successful next week?

PERSONAL

WEEKLY FOCUS:

WEEKLY GOAL:

PROFESSIONAL

WEEKLY FOCUS:

WEEKLY GOAL:

Honor Your Roles

TIPS FOR *Teachers*

Delegate responsibilities. Designate roles and responsibilities in your class. Rotate these jobs among students. You know the jobs: pass back papers, collect papers, turn on the computers, set up the DVD, clean the board, and whatever else helps you get things done without doing it all yourself. One caution: some responsibilities, such as taking attendance and grading each others' tests, potentially have legal repercussions.

TIPS FOR *Teaching*

Use think-alouds. Think-alouds allow others to see *what* you think as you narrate *how* you think while reading a text or discussing an idea. Think-aloud strategies are not a sequence but a set of habits of mind common to all effective learners that can help students make sense of a wide variety of problems and texts. When we use the think-aloud technique, we predict, describe, compare, connect, monitor and correct, question, clarify, apply previous or new knowledge, identify what's important, troubleshoot, and speculate.

MONDAY 25

TUESDAY 26

WEDNESDAY 27

The Teacher's Daybook by Jim Burke (Heinemann: Portsmouth, NH); © 2012 by Jim Burke.

TIPS FOR *Professional Learning*

engage

COLLABORATE. Look for ways to share the load. Instead of working into the night on your own, arrange to meet with teachers who use the same book or teach the same material. Put your heads together to create better lesson plans, in less time, that meet the needs of all your students. Be sure to invite the new and struggling teachers into your group. They need your wisdom, your friendship, and your example. If you can't find time to meet, plan, or discuss at school, work on-line—through email or Google Docs (www.google.com).

Weekly Reflections

On a scale of 1–10, gauge (a) *how effective you were as a teacher this week, and* (b) *how you are feeling this week*. What adjective might best capture your teaching and your feelings this week?

THURSDAY 28

FRIDAY 1

REMINDERS · NOTES · WEEKEND HOMEWORK

plan ahead

▶ How does next week relate to this week?

▶ What continues to confuse or frustrate your students?

▶ Think of your class as a story: What should happen next?

▶ Who can help you be more successful next week?

PERSONAL

WEEKLY FOCUS:

WEEKLY GOAL:

PROFESSIONAL

WEEKLY FOCUS:

WEEKLY GOAL:

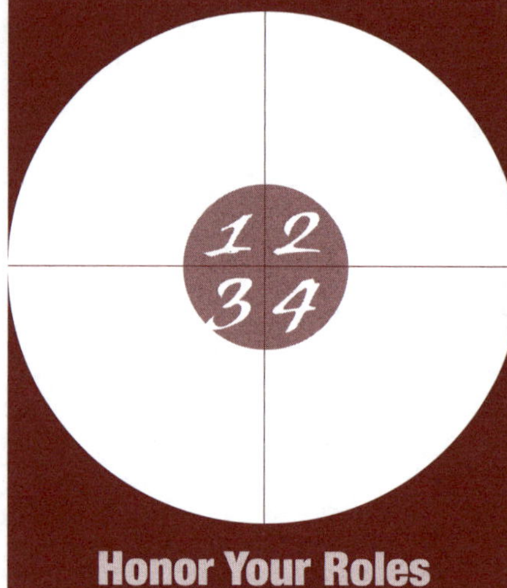

Honor Your Roles

TIPS FOR *Teachers*

Get help. Request student aids. Create a list of ways parents can help; ask them to sign up for whatever they are willing to do at Back to School Night. The list might include handling book orders, leading Junior Great Books sessions, going on field trips, volunteering in the classroom, preparing materials for the next day's activities. Ask local organizations and businesses for help with mentors and tutors. Don't neglect the gifts of older students who can be tutors and aides.

TIPS FOR *Teaching*

Make predictions. Predicting means making a guess about what will happen next or later based on your interpretations. Predicting is an essential habit to develop in all students. Model how you use this habit when working by thinking aloud during an assignment. Interrupt students at work and ask them what will happen next based on all they know at this time. Press further to find out why they think that.

MONDAY 4

TUESDAY 5

WEDNESDAY 6

TIPS FOR *Professional Learning*

BRANCH OUT. It is surprising how much reading about another field of study can help us better understand our own. Another option is to invite some colleagues from other departments to meet with your Circle of Friends; such cross-fertilization can only be good for you, the school, and your students.

toss

Weekly Reflections

On a scale of 1–10, gauge (a) *how effective you were as a teacher this week, and* (b) *how you are feeling this week*. What adjective might best capture your teaching and your feelings this week?

THURSDAY 7

FRIDAY 8

REMINDERS · NOTES · WEEKEND HOMEWORK

plan ahead

- How does next week relate to this week?
- What continues to confuse or frustrate your students?
- Think of your class as a story: What should happen next?
- Who can help you be more successful next week?

The Teacher's Daybook by Jim Burke (Heinemann: Portsmouth, NH); © 2012 by Jim Burke.

PERSONAL

WEEKLY FOCUS:

WEEKLY GOAL:

PROFESSIONAL

WEEKLY FOCUS:

WEEKLY GOAL:

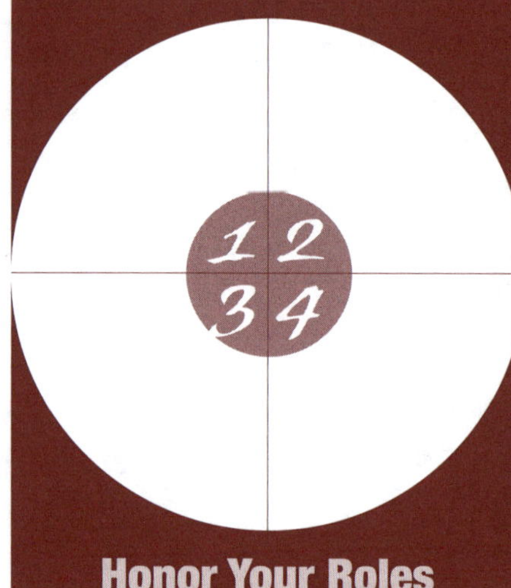

Honor Your Roles

TIPS FOR *Teachers*

Dress for comfort *and* respect. This doesn't mean you have to wear a suit and a tie, but it does mean you want to be taken seriously. Wearing shorts and T-shirts, unless you coach athletics, will cost you respect in the eyes of your students. A clean, comfortable, but professional outfit will let students know you take your work seriously and want the respect a professional deserves.

TIPS FOR *Teaching*

Take good notes. Taking good notes is not only an essential skill but a useful habit. Taking notes makes students more active learners, forcing them to evaluate whether information is important enough to write down. While you or others read aloud, for example, students can take notes to help them listen more closely and minimize distracting behaviors. In short, notetaking is one of the most useful strategies and skills students can use to record, organize, remember, and respond to what they read. Teach them also how to take notes from a video.

MONDAY 11

TUESDAY 12

WEDNESDAY 13

TIPS FOR *Professional Learning*

REVISIT YOUR STATE STANDARDS. Aside from testing, you have subject-specific standards you are supposed to address in your classes. Before the year is up, review the standards for your subject(s) and reflect on which ones your students effectively mastered and which ones you need to better address in the year ahead. Think about what you can do over the summer to better prepare your students to meet those standards next year. Discuss your ideas and your feelings with your Circle of Friends.

renew

Weekly Reflections

On a scale of 1–10, gauge (a) *how effective you were as a teacher this week, and* (b) *how you are feeling this week*. What adjective might best capture your teaching and your feelings this week?

THURSDAY 14

FRIDAY 15

REMINDERS · NOTES · WEEKEND HOMEWORK

plan ahead

- How does next week relate to this week?
- What continues to confuse or frustrate your students?
- Think of your class as a story: What should happen next?
- Who can help you be more successful next week?

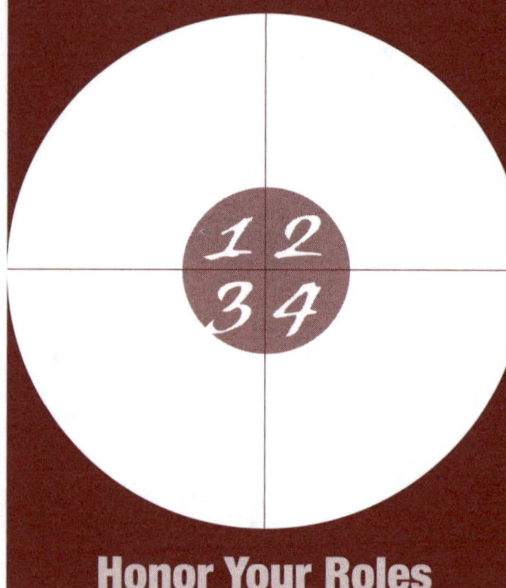

Honor Your Roles

TIPS FOR *Teachers*

Anticipate absences. Designate a place near the door of your class (if possible) where students can pick up copies of assignments they missed or might have lost. This prevents students from surrounding you as you try to get ready to teach. You might have dated folders into which you place extra copies of handouts. Teach students to see you later or ask at an appropriate time about what they missed.

TIPS FOR *Teaching*

Retell the text. Retelling texts teaches students to identify what is crucial in the text and how the sequence of that information determines its meaning. The activity challenges them to remember information and events, making them interact with the information from a variety of perspectives: their own, their audience's, and the author's. Finally, retelling is its own form of assessment, since their performance confirms that they read the assignment.

MONDAY 18

TUESDAY 19

WEDNESDAY 20

TIPS FOR *Professional Learning*

THE STORY OF YOUR YEAR. Think of your year as a story, one with a cast of characters, a plot, different themes, inevitable conflicts, most of which were resolved, and various surprises along the way. As the author of this story, how would you like it to end in the months ahead? What can you do to accomplish that ending? What is most memorable about this year's story? Tell this story to your Circle of Friends. Thank them for being such essential characters in the story of your year.

experience

Weekly Reflections

On a scale of 1–10, gauge (a) *how effective you were as a teacher this week, and* (b) *how you are feeling this week*. What adjective might best capture your teaching and your feelings this week?

THURSDAY 21

FRIDAY 22

REMINDERS · NOTES · WEEKEND HOMEWORK

plan ahead

▸ How does next week relate to this week?

▸ What continues to confuse or frustrate your students?

▸ Think of your class as a story: What should happen next?

▸ Who can help you be more successful next week?

PERSONAL

WEEKLY FOCUS:

WEEKLY GOAL:

PROFESSIONAL

WEEKLY FOCUS:

WEEKLY GOAL:

Honor Your Roles

TIPS FOR *Teachers*

Recycle. Reuse. Most schools have very tight budgets when it comes to photocopying, in part due to the high cost of paper. Copy only a few extra handouts. Also decide ahead of time if you can collect the handouts when students finish so you can reuse them next year. Take all old handouts or other one-sided papers and cut each into four equal-sized pieces. Keep these handy for everything from passes to quizzes, notes to activities.

TIPS FOR *Teaching*

Draw the action. Have individuals or groups use paper or transparencies to "publish" their visual explanations on the overhead or the walls, making an informal presentation of their work. Have them explain what they were trying to accomplish through their visual explanation of the story, the process, the concept.

MONDAY 25

TUESDAY 26

WEDNESDAY 27

TIPS FOR *Professional Learning*

THINK IN THREES. So often we engage in either/or thinking. Instead of yes/no thinking, try thinking in threes: students/parents/school, past/present/future, advanced/middle/struggling students, hear/watch/ touch what they learn, and so on. Brainstorm possible applications of this idea with members of your Circle, or discuss the results of their efforts to incorporate these ideas.

participate

Weekly Reflections

On a scale of 1–10, gauge (a) *how effective you were as a teacher this week, and* (b) *how you are feeling this week*. What adjective might best capture your teaching and your feelings this week?

THURSDAY 28

FRIDAY 29

REMINDERS · NOTES · WEEKEND HOMEWORK

plan ahead

➤ How does next week relate to this week?

➤ What continues to confuse or frustrate your students?

➤ Think of your class as a story: What should happen next?

➤ Who can help you be more successful next week?

PERSONAL

WEEKLY FOCUS:

WEEKLY GOAL:

PROFESSIONAL

WEEKLY FOCUS:

WEEKLY GOAL:

Honor Your Roles

TIPS FOR *Teachers*

Save money on ink and paper. When you are finished creating that assignment or other school-related document, don't print it up at home. Instead, email it to yourself as an attachment and use the school's paper and ink, saving you time and money.

TIPS FOR *Teaching*

Read different types of text. Good readers read a text in different ways; they also read a variety of types of text (e.g., poetic, literary, informational). Students must develop the same capacities, reading texts of different types and levels of difficulty. They must learn when, how, and why to adopt new strategies while reading; indeed they must learn that different types of text require different or at least adjusted reading strategies depending on the demands they make on the reader.

MONDAY 1

TUESDAY 2

WEDNESDAY 3

TIPS FOR *Professional Learning*

RENEW YOURSELF. This is always both an exciting and a demanding period of the year. Suddenly there seems to be so little time, and so much to do. Now is a good time to step away from your work for an afternoon or a Saturday to gather the strength you need for the homestretch. Go to a museum or take a walk or a bike ride. Go to a symphony or a new restaurant. Play a game of tennis or a long game of Monopoly with your family one night. Look to your Circle for ideas, support, and energy.

appreciate

Weekly Reflections

On a scale of 1–10, gauge (a) *how effective you were as a teacher this week, and* (b) *how you are feeling this week*. What adjective might best capture your teaching and your feelings this week?

THURSDAY 4

FRIDAY 5

REMINDERS · NOTES · WEEKEND HOMEWORK

plan ahead

▶ How does next week relate to this week?

▶ What continues to confuse or frustrate your students?

▶ Think of your class as a story: What should happen next?

▶ Who can help you be more successful next week?

PERSONAL

WEEKLY FOCUS:

WEEKLY GOAL:

PROFESSIONAL

WEEKLY FOCUS:

WEEKLY GOAL:

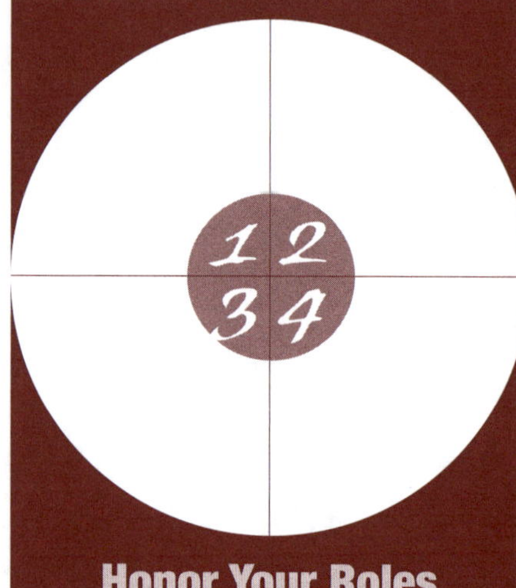

Honor Your Roles

TIPS FOR *Teachers*

Get a good clipboard. An active teacher is moving all around the room. You need to be able to bring a desk with you when you move around or conference with students. The ideal clipboard is longer than average—about fourteen inches—which allows you to attach sticky notes and sticky flags on the bottom space. Some clipboards come with calculators at the top, a nice feature for science and math teachers. Be sure your clipboard opens up to reveal a space where you can put extra supplies or completed evaluation forms.

TIPS FOR *Teaching*

Write to improve understanding. No reading of a text is complete until readers make their own text. This might be done in any of a number of ways: discussing what they read, translating the ideas into some visual explanation or response, or writing. Students might write to summarize or clarify, or even to extend their thinking about the text. Writing is inherently active; to write is to think.

MONDAY 8

TUESDAY 9

WEDNESDAY 10

The Teacher's Daybook by Jim Burke (Heinemann: Portsmouth, NH); © 2012 by Jim Burke.

balance

TIPS FOR *Professional Learning*

THINK AHEAD. Begin thinking about the time ahead when you will again have time. Summer break is not far. It is a time for renewal, for projects, classes, adventures, family, and friends. Ask colleagues what they are doing, if they have places or experiences to recommend. Begin gathering information so you have something to look forward to and are ready when the time comes. Consider applying for a summer fellowship with the National Endowment for the Humanities (www.neh.gov). Set up a date with your Circle of Friends to have a nice dinner to look forward to when the year ends.

Weekly Reflections

On a scale of 1–10, gauge (a) *how effective you were as a teacher this week, and* (b) *how you are feeling this week*. What adjective might best capture your teaching and your feelings this week?

THURSDAY 11

FRIDAY 12

REMINDERS · NOTES · WEEKEND HOMEWORK

plan ahead

- How does next week relate to this week?
- What continues to confuse or frustrate your students?
- Think of your class as a story: What should happen next?
- Who can help you be more successful next week?

PERSONAL

WEEKLY FOCUS:

WEEKLY GOAL:

PROFESSIONAL

WEEKLY FOCUS:

WEEKLY GOAL:

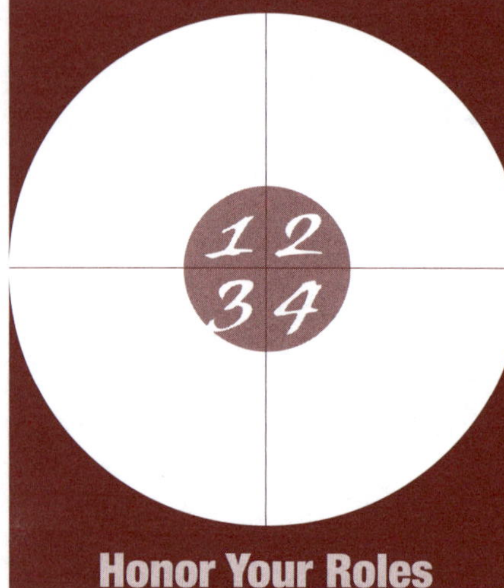

Honor Your Roles

TIPS FOR *Teachers*

Keep copies at school and at home. Keep an extra copy of the class roster, complete with students' phone numbers, at home in case you need to reach a parent. Also, keep copies of such things as the school/district directory both at home and at school, as well as any emergency phone tree. It can be convenient to have a copy of your union contract at home and at school, too.

TIPS FOR *Teaching*

Think from a variety of perspectives. Literature offers us the chance to see the world through the eyes of The Other. This might mean that a man reads a book written about a woman or from a woman's perspective, or a younger student reads one written from the point of view of a senior citizen. It doesn't just apply to literature; science and history, health and business classes offer the same opportunities to think imaginatively. Such imaginative thinking, if cultivated, enables students to appreciate and understand their subject at a much deeper level.

MONDAY 15

TUESDAY 16

WEDNESDAY 17

TIPS FOR *Professional Learning*

imagine

EVIDENCE OF SUCCESS. As the year's end comes in sight, you begin to wonder what you have accomplished, what difference your efforts have made. Take time to think about or even make a list of the kids you've helped, the programs you've started, the difference you've made in your classroom and the school. Take yourself out to a nice place where you can review your goals and principles, and reflect on how you've improved, what you've done. Share these accomplishments and insights with your Circle of Friends.

Weekly Reflections

On a scale of 1–10, gauge (a) *how effective you were as a teacher this week, and* (b) *how you are feeling this week*. What adjective might best capture your teaching and your feelings this week?

THURSDAY 18

FRIDAY 19

REMINDERS · NOTES · WEEKEND HOMEWORK

plan ahead

▸ How does next week relate to this week?

▸ What continues to confuse or frustrate your students?

▸ Think of your class as a story: What should happen next?

▸ Who can help you be more successful next week?

PERSONAL

WEEKLY FOCUS:

WEEKLY GOAL:

PROFESSIONAL

WEEKLY FOCUS:

WEEKLY GOAL:

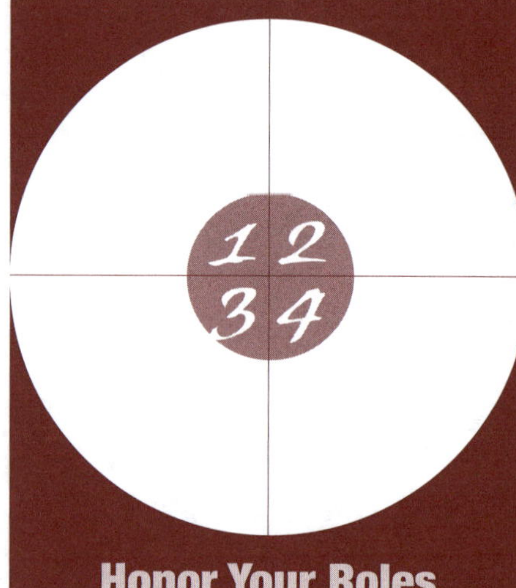

Honor Your Roles

TIPS FOR *Teachers*

Document concerns. If you see something that raises a red flag or if you make what seems like a mistake, write down what happened, who was involved, when it happened, and where it took place. Then consult whomever you trust and think most appropriate. If it is obvious that you should go to the administration or should talk to a counselor about something serious, consider asking a trusted colleague to accompany you.

TIPS FOR *Teaching*

Develop students' prior knowledge. If we take time before to develop or access knowledge, we will read a text faster, be more engaged, understand it better, and remember it longer. Obviously, we *have* to know certain things if we are to understand what we study. Helping students realize this and understand the different types of prior knowledge that can help them is one of the most important lessons we can help them learn.

MONDAY 22

TUESDAY 23

WEDNESDAY 24

The Teacher's Daybook by Jim Burke (Heinemann: Portsmouth, NH); © 2012 by Jim Burke.

TIPS FOR *Professional Learning*

WHAT ARE YOUR GIFTS? Every year teachers face different and, almost inevitably, new demands that were not there when they entered the field. Thus we must continually ask ourselves "What are my gifts?" and "How can I make the best use of these gifts to benefit the most people?" Discuss with your Circle what your gifts are and how else you might be able to use them around school.

contribute

Weekly Reflections

On a scale of 1–10, gauge (a) *how effective you were as a teacher this week, and* (b) *how you are feeling this week*. What adjective might best capture your teaching and your feelings this week?

THURSDAY 25

FRIDAY 26

REMINDERS · NOTES · WEEKEND HOMEWORK

plan ahead

▸ How does next week relate to this week?

▸ What continues to confuse or frustrate your students?

▸ Think of your class as a story: What should happen next?

▸ Who can help you be more successful next week?

PERSONAL

WEEKLY FOCUS:

WEEKLY GOAL:

PROFESSIONAL

WEEKLY FOCUS:

WEEKLY GOAL:

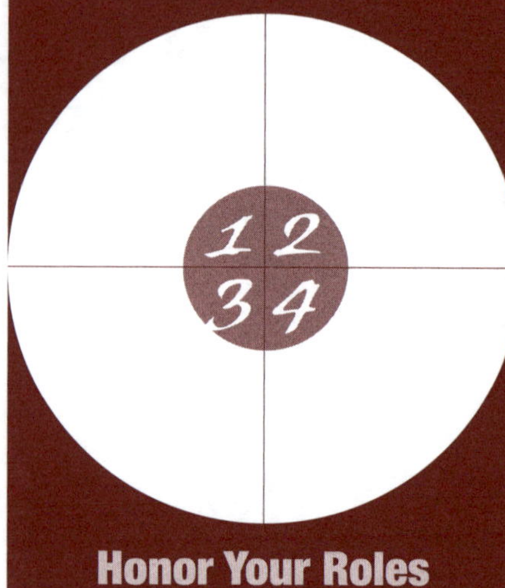

Honor Your Roles

TIPS FOR *Teachers*

Think ahead. As vacation nears: Lock up or take home what you cannot risk losing. Ask if it's okay if you take your classroom computer home to work with it over the summer. Bring home those books and materials you want to use when you begin planning for next year. Keep examples of student work that will be useful next year. Keep an eye out for cast-off books and school materials you can use in your classes for the fall.

TIPS FOR *Teaching*

Summarize and paraphrase. The ability to summarize information is crucial for adult success in most fields. Being able to take an entire article, book, or process and sum it up in a sentence or a short paragraph demonstrates understanding. This active process whereby the reader extracts the main idea(s) and sums up their importance becomes a habit in more proficient readers. It is not a skill we are born with, however; good summaries must be precise and contain specific types of information that the novice often overlooks.

MONDAY 29

TUESDAY 30

WEDNESDAY 1

TIPS FOR *Professional Learning*

FAITH IN TEACHING. Teaching is an act of faith—in humanity, our future, our own ability, and that of our students. We see the children do what no one thought they could. We see the progress others cannot or did not think was possible. Reflect on your own faith and what sustains you as a teacher and person during the difficult times. Discuss your own ideas and the role of faith in your work with your Circle of Friends. To further explore this important subject, consider reading *Teaching with Fire: Poems That Sustain the Courage to Teach* (Intrator and Scribner).

Weekly Reflections

On a scale of 1–10, gauge (a) *how effective you were as a teacher this week, and* (b) *how you are feeling this week*. What adjective might best capture your teaching and your feelings this week?

THURSDAY 2

FRIDAY 3

REMINDERS · NOTES · WEEKEND HOMEWORK

plan ahead

▸ How does next week relate to this week?

▸ What continues to confuse or frustrate your students?

▸ Think of your class as a story: What should happen next?

▸ Who can help you be more successful next week?

PERSONAL

WEEKLY FOCUS:

WEEKLY GOAL:

PROFESSIONAL

WEEKLY FOCUS:

WEEKLY GOAL:

Honor Your Roles

TIPS FOR *Teachers*

Thank people. The secretaries and plant managers, the aides and the assistants all make life easier for you. The gratitude you show now will ensure that you can get into your class after hours or get that emergency copy made when you need it. Keep a pack of blank note cards at school to drop quick thank-yous to the people who do things for you.

TIPS FOR *Teaching*

Expand students' vocabulary. Expand students' vocabulary using the following strategies. Read, read, read: this is the single best way to expand vocabulary. Word walls: keep a running display of words you have introduced so they can be referred to or reviewed by students. Semantic maps: put the word in the middle, then add branches for the definition, the part of speech, a picture, and three examples. Modeling: use the words you teach along with challenging but useful words when speaking in class. Reinforce the benefits of precise language.

MONDAY 6

TUESDAY 7

WEDNESDAY 8

TIPS FOR *Professional Learning*

SEEK LAUGHTER. Your work is stressful, even if you love it. The numbers, the demands, the changes—all of which are beyond your control. Take yourself out to a play or watch a movie you are sure will make you laugh. If you don't like movies, get together with friends and tell stories, play Pictionary, read the *New Yorker* for its cartoons, or do whatever else works for you.

clarify

Weekly Reflections

On a scale of 1–10, gauge (a) *how effective you were as a teacher this week, and* (b) *how you are feeling this week*. What adjective might best capture your teaching and your feelings this week?

THURSDAY 9

FRIDAY 10

REMINDERS · NOTES · WEEKEND HOMEWORK

plan ahead

- How does next week relate to this week?
- What continues to confuse or frustrate your students?
- Think of your class as a story: What should happen next?
- Who can help you be more successful next week?

PERSONAL

WEEKLY FOCUS:

WEEKLY GOAL:

PROFESSIONAL

WEEKLY FOCUS:

WEEKLY GOAL:

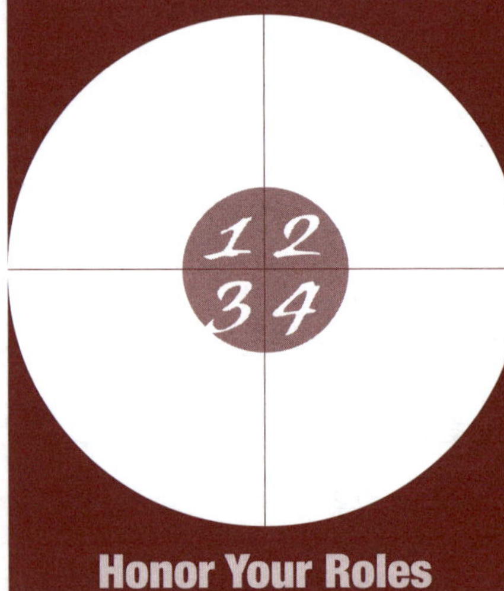

Honor Your Roles

TIPS FOR *Teachers*

Take home some books. Whether these are just novels you want to read or textbooks you should review or even teach, take home a copy for the summer. This will save you a trip in August and a few dollars, too, if you would end up buying these books otherwise. Be sure, as you go, that you have books set up that you want to read, for personal and professional pleasure, in the months ahead.

TIPS FOR *Teaching*

Make the foreign familiar. First, determine why the information or ideas are unfamiliar. Are the words from a different language, specialized terms from a discipline you do not know, or in a story the likes of which you have never heard before? Find the familiar within the foreign by asking: What might I compare this to? Does this remind me of anything with which I am already familiar? Can I compare this to any experiences of my own? What word might have an equivalent meaning?

MONDAY 13

TUESDAY 14

WEDNESDAY 15

The Teacher's Daybook by Jim Burke (Heinemann: Portsmouth, NH); © 2012 by Jim Burke.

limit

TIPS FOR *Professional Learning*

DEAR STUDENTS. The engaged, reflective teacher learns as much if not more than the students—and from students—during a year. Write a letter to your students in which you tell them what you learned from them and what they mean to you. Thank them and give them the chance to thank you by asking them to write their own letter in response to yours. Share your letter with your Circle of Friends, using it to discuss all that you learned from them during the course of this year.

Weekly Reflections

On a scale of 1–10, gauge (a) *how effective you were as a teacher this week,* and (b) *how you are feeling this week*. What adjective might best capture your teaching and your feelings this week?

THURSDAY 16

FRIDAY 17

REMINDERS · NOTES · WEEKEND HOMEWORK

plan ahead

- How does next week relate to this week?
- What continues to confuse or frustrate your students?
- Think of your class as a story: What should happen next?
- Who can help you be more successful next week?

Honor Your Roles

TIPS FOR *Teachers*

Reduce distractions. Hang a sheet of paper from your door; late students can sign in there, so you can keep focused on teaching. Put a clip by the door for notices and attendance sheets to be picked up quickly and quietly. Turn down the ringer on your classroom phone and the sound on your classroom computer (headphones can also be used). Put a curtain or paper over your classroom door window. Erase unnecessary stuff from the board.

TIPS FOR *Teaching*

Improve speed, fluency, and stamina. Successful students are able to work and read with reasonable fluency and speed. Fluency involves their ability to make sense of different aspects and keep moving at a productive pace. Stamina further distinguishes strong from developing thinkers. Stamina, an essential capacity, ensures that students can maintain attention over a long period of time. Such capacities are of vital importance when taking tests or doing work that requires sustained attention over an extended period of time.

MONDAY 20

TUESDAY 21

WEDNESDAY 22

TIPS FOR *Professional Learning*

SET SUMMER GOALS. What do you want to accomplish by summer's end? What do you want to have read, done, or seen? Before departing for the summer, schedule a date with your Circle of Friends for the week before school starts. Do this now, and make a commitment to do something—read, go, learn—you can all discuss when you return.

Weekly Reflections

On a scale of 1–10, gauge (a) *how effective you were as a teacher this week, and* (b) *how you are feeling this week*. What adjective might best capture your teaching and your feelings this week?

THURSDAY 23

FRIDAY 24

REMINDERS · NOTES · WEEKEND HOMEWORK

plan ahead

- How does next week relate to this week?
- What continues to confuse or frustrate your students?
- Think of your class as a story: What should happen next?
- Who can help you be more successful next week?

PERSONAL

WEEKLY FOCUS:

WEEKLY GOAL:

PROFESSIONAL

WEEKLY FOCUS:

WEEKLY GOAL:

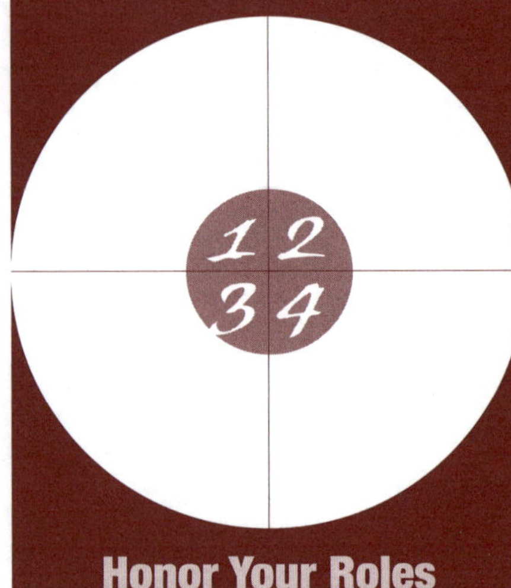

Honor Your Roles

TIPS FOR *Teachers*

Clean up, then check out. Before you stop working for the night, or before you leave your classroom, clean up your work space. Recycle or toss what you can. Put away files and supplies. It only takes a minute and you will find a calm space when you return in the morning. Psychologically it helps to put one day away and come in knowing you can start fresh the next day.

TIPS FOR *Teaching*

Determine what is important. Teach students to identify what is important by directing their attention to certain words, phrases, sections, or aspects of the text that you think merit scrutiny. Teach them to recognize what is important and where to find it. Try the following: ask them to look for specific information (words, ideas, structures); model and explain how you read the same text and find the important information.

MONDAY 27

TUESDAY 28

WEDNESDAY 29

forgive

CATCH UP. Get all those projects out of the way that have piled up over the last nine months or so. Give yourself over to them completely so you can move on to the other things you want to do. Catch up on other things that might have fallen behind, also: correspondence, reading, talking to your children and spouse, cleaning out the garage, washing the car.

Weekly Reflections

On a scale of 1–10, gauge (a) *how effective you were as a teacher this week, and* (b) *how you are feeling this week*. What adjective might best capture your teaching and your feelings this week?

THURSDAY 30

FRIDAY 31

REMINDERS · NOTES · WEEKEND HOMEWORK

plan ahead

> How does next week relate to this week?

> What continues to confuse or frustrate your students?

> Think of your class as a story: What should happen next?

> Who can help you be more successful next week?

PERSONAL

WEEKLY FOCUS:

WEEKLY GOAL:

PROFESSIONAL

WEEKLY FOCUS:

WEEKLY GOAL:

Honor Your Roles

TIPS FOR *Teachers*

Purge the papers. Whether it is the end of the first week or the end of another school year, you have papers, catalogs, and memos everywhere you turn. Go through your files, drawers, and cabinets and purge anything that you can find online or in the department or main office. If you don't have time to read it or file it, toss it. If it's a duplicate, toss it. If it's not current or relevant to what you are or will be teaching, toss it.

TIPS FOR *Teaching*

Explain their thinking: elaboration strategies. The most important device for the teacher is the well-phrased, timely question. Pose questions to help students clarify and evaluate their ideas prior to elaborating on them: "I think I understand what you're saying, Jane, and it sounds like a potentially incredible insight. Can you think of another way of saying that or find an example in the text to help us better see what you mean?" or "Why do you think that's such an important piece of information?"

MONDAY 3

TUESDAY 4

WEDNESDAY 5

TIPS FOR *Professional Learning*

CHALLENGE YOURSELF. Take on some new projects or choose to do something new. Your summer months are one of the rewards for all the work you've done the last nine months or so. Make the most of them!

express

Weekly Reflections

On a scale of 1–10, gauge (a) *how effective you were as a teacher this week, and* (b) *how you are feeling this week*. What adjective might best capture your teaching and your feelings this week?

THURSDAY 6

FRIDAY 7

REMINDERS · NOTES · WEEKEND HOMEWORK

plan ahead

▸ How does next week relate to this week?

▸ What continues to confuse or frustrate your students?

▸ Think of your class as a story: What should happen next?

▸ Who can help you be more successful next week?

PERSONAL

WEEKLY FOCUS:

WEEKLY GOAL:

PROFESSIONAL

WEEKLY FOCUS:

WEEKLY GOAL:

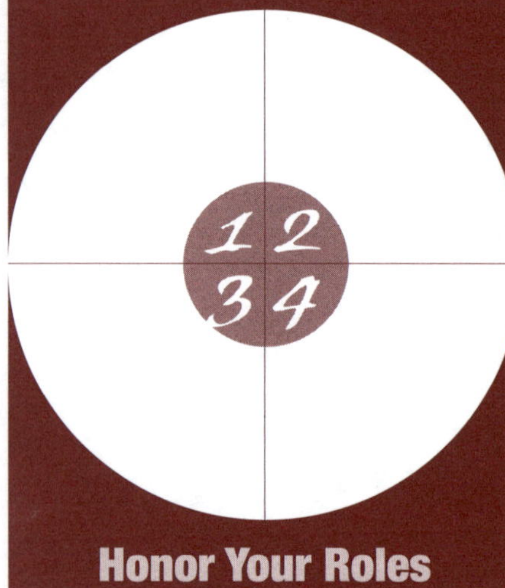

Honor Your Roles

TIPS FOR *Teachers*

Name that file! Organize documents in ways that make sense for what you teach. Name folders with nouns: "Calculator Basics" or "Lab Procedures." Give some files very generic names like "Reading Lists"; others need more specific names. Use multiple names with categories like "India": "India: Politics," "India: Culture." Add other folders for more general use: "Writing Topics" or "School Business." Hanging files are better than file folders. Alphabetize. Avoid color coding; it becomes difficult to maintain.

TIPS FOR *Teaching*

Discuss their reading: reporting strategies. The absence of reporting strategies, which often depend on language or structures specific to a discipline, can often impede the development of struggling readers who feel unprepared both to read and to discuss what they read. Teachers need to help students develop these vocabularies and strategies through direct teaching, opportunity to practice them, and, most important, modeling.

MONDAY 10

TUESDAY 11

WEDNESDAY 12

notice

TIPS FOR *Professional Learning*

GET AWAY. On a daily basis, get away for a bike ride or a hike. Take advantage of being able to travel during the week. Make the trips special, taking a trip with just one of your children or even one of your parents. Seek those places and experiences that will renew and inspire.

Weekly Reflections

On a scale of 1–10, gauge (a) *how effective you were as a teacher this week, and* (b) *how you are feeling this week*. What adjective might best capture your teaching and your feelings this week?

THURSDAY 13

FRIDAY 14

REMINDERS · NOTES · WEEKEND HOMEWORK

plan ahead

▸ How does next week relate to this week?

▸ What continues to confuse or frustrate your students?

▸ Think of your class as a story: What should happen next?

▸ Who can help you be more successful next week?

PERSONAL

WEEKLY FOCUS:

WEEKLY GOAL:

PROFESSIONAL

WEEKLY FOCUS:

WEEKLY GOAL:

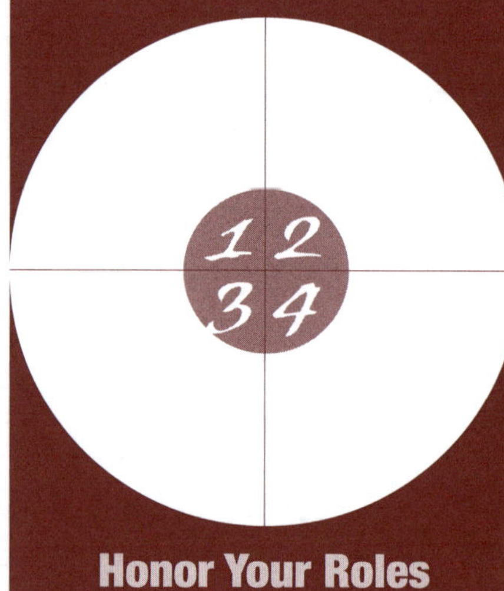

Honor Your Roles

TIPS FOR *Teachers*

Do less, accomplish more. You never have time to go through your entire file cabinet to purge old files. You do have five minutes a day to go through as many as you can; you can even set a timer to keep yourself from going overboard. Keep only single copies of any document. You will accomplish more this way because you will move through it all. Guinness lists a man who ate an entire car, one little piece at a time. Of course, you should use the time you save for more healthy pursuits.

TIPS FOR *Teaching*

Make the abstract concrete. As experts we forget how complicated some texts and ideas can be for students. Some students consistently struggle to make sense of abstractions encountered in texts. Abstract material challenges them in every subject area, whether it is the abstraction of "health" or concepts such as freedom, power, or gravity. Students need help learning to identify and understand these abstractions as they move into more sophisticated ideas and texts in all subject areas.

grow

TIPS FOR *Professional Learning*

BEGIN PROJECTS. Try to choose projects with clear and reasonable endings to them. You might, for example, paint or redecorate a room, or you might refinish a piece of furniture or complete that scrapbook with all those pictures you've taken during the past year.

Weekly Reflections

On a scale of 1–10, gauge (a) *how effective you were as a teacher this week, and* (b) *how you are feeling this week*. What adjective might best capture your teaching and your feelings this week?

THURSDAY 20

FRIDAY 21

REMINDERS · NOTES · WEEKEND HOMEWORK

plan ahead

▶ How does next week relate to this week?

▶ What continues to confuse or frustrate your students?

▶ Think of your class as a story: What should happen next?

▶ Who can help you be more successful next week?

PERSONAL

WEEKLY FOCUS:

WEEKLY GOAL:

PROFESSIONAL

WEEKLY FOCUS:

WEEKLY GOAL:

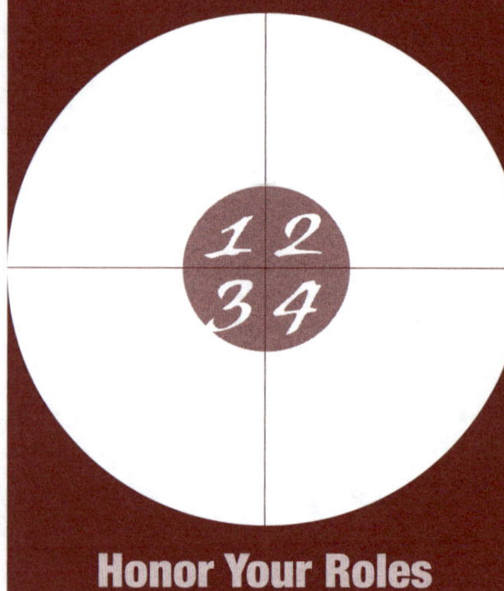

Honor Your Roles

TIPS FOR *Teachers*

Let your computer help you. Create a set of templates of frequently used documents. For example, create a checklist you can give to students who want you to write letters of recommendation. Or create a writing scoring rubric that you can revise quickly to meet the needs of a particular assignment without having to reinvent (and rewrite) the entire document. Instead of typing up some texts, go online and see if you can find them there; then cut and paste them into your document and spend your time formatting for improved instruction.

TIPS FOR *Teaching*

Stop and reflect periodically. We get so busy, it is hard to remember to stop, look, and listen: Are we doing all that we should to help our students and ourselves? Are we reaching all students or just the ones who always seem to "get it"? How much work are students actually doing in a week? Are students reading a variety of types of text? How long do our assignments take to complete? How are we using information to improve teaching and learning?

MONDAY 24

TUESDAY 25

WEDNESDAY 26

try

TIPS FOR *Professional Learning*

LOOKING BACK, LOOKING AHEAD. As hard as it is to believe, another school year will soon end. Reflect on your past year and jot down some hopes for the year ahead while this year is still fresh in your mind. Think about what worked and what did not, what you improved and what you want to improve for the year ahead. Think about what you can do during the summer months ahead to help you achieve these possible goals. Write a note of thanks to the members of your Circle of Friends.

Weekly Reflections

On a scale of 1–10, gauge (a) *how effective you were as a teacher this week, and* (b) *how you are feeling this week*. What adjective might best capture your teaching and your feelings this week?

THURSDAY 27

FRIDAY 28

REMINDERS · NOTES · WEEKEND HOMEWORK

plan ahead

- How does next week relate to this week?
- What continues to confuse or frustrate your students?
- Think of your class as a story: What should happen next?
- Who can help you be more successful next week?

PERSONAL

WEEKLY FOCUS:

WEEKLY GOAL:

PROFESSIONAL

WEEKLY FOCUS:

WEEKLY GOAL:

Honor Your Roles

TIPS FOR *Teachers*

Set and know your limits. Divide larger workloads or tasks into smaller units. Set goals: if I get five papers done, I can watch that show. Use a timer or the alarm on your computer, then say: I will get as many done in the next hour as I can and then work in the garden or read the paper.

TIPS FOR *Teaching*

Develop students' confidence. Nothing distinguishes successful students more than their capacity and willingness to persevere in the face of failure. They know if they work at it, understanding will come, though they may need to employ a number of strategies until they find the right one. Struggling students tend not to trust their interpretation or solution, even if it is correct. Experienced learners recognize when, where, or why they are having trouble; they then adjust their strategies as needed.

MONDAY 1

TUESDAY 2

WEDNESDAY 3

TIPS FOR *Professional Learning*

CONSIDER TAKING A SUMMER WORKSHOP OR ONLINE COURSE. Many of these are very social as well as educational. Consider signing up to attend one in a nice place with someone from your Circle.

respect

Weekly Reflections

On a scale of 1–10, gauge (a) *how effective you were as a teacher this week,* and (b) *how you are feeling this week*. What adjective might best capture your teaching and your feelings this week?

THURSDAY 4

FRIDAY 5

REMINDERS · NOTES · WEEKEND HOMEWORK

plan ahead

- How does next week relate to this week?
- What continues to confuse or frustrate your students?
- Think of your class as a story: What should happen next?
- Who can help you be more successful next week?

PERSONAL

WEEKLY FOCUS:

WEEKLY GOAL:

PROFESSIONAL

WEEKLY FOCUS:

WEEKLY GOAL:

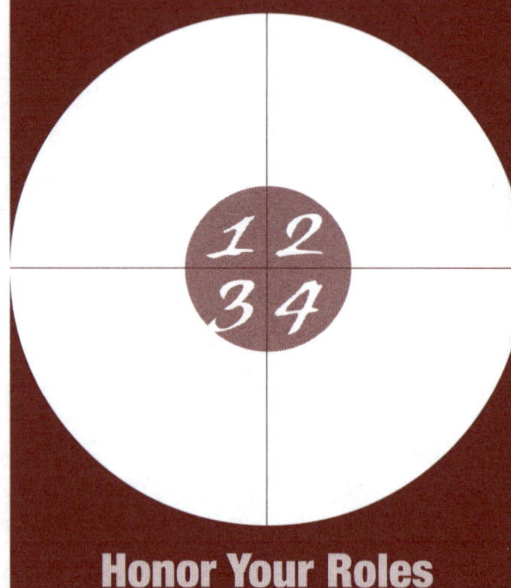

Honor Your Roles

TIPS FOR *Teachers*

Know where you work best . . . and work there. Some teachers have fewer distractions in their classroom after school than they would at home. Some find themselves unable to concentrate at school and thus get less done. Have a designated, well-lit space where you can work without distraction; stock that space with all the supplies you need and a comfortable, ergonomic chair.

TIPS FOR *Teaching*

Review, reflect, reinforce. As students finish an assignment, they can do several things to improve their understanding and ensure the gains they've made last. Providing opportunities to reflect on what they learned, how they worked, and what the assignment was about helps reinforce both understanding and the skills they developed.

MONDAY 8

TUESDAY 9

WEDNESDAY 10

TIPS FOR *Professional Learning*

LEARN NEW THINGS. These need not have anything to do with school. In fact it's probably best if they don't. Whether you take a class in painting, learn how to use a new computer program, or go to lectures at the local library or museum, these learning experiences will enrich your life. Interesting people make interesting teachers.

risk

Weekly Reflections

On a scale of 1–10, gauge (a) *how effective you were as a teacher this week, and* (b) *how you are feeling this week*. What adjective might best capture your teaching and your feelings this week?

THURSDAY 11

FRIDAY 12

REMINDERS · NOTES · WEEKEND HOMEWORK

plan ahead

➤ How does next week relate to this week?

➤ What continues to confuse or frustrate your students?

➤ Think of your class as a story: What should happen next?

➤ Who can help you be more successful next week?

127

PERSONAL

WEEKLY FOCUS:

WEEKLY GOAL:

PROFESSIONAL

WEEKLY FOCUS:

WEEKLY GOAL:

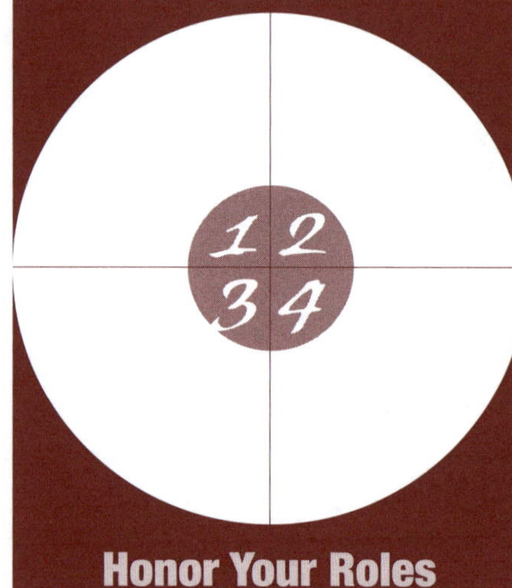

Honor Your Roles

TIPS FOR *Teachers*

Determine the order of your operations. If you have thirty-five papers, some will require more attention than others. If you are preparing a big project, some aspects of that work will demand more of your time and attention than others. Sort through the tasks or papers to organize them (easiest to hardest or vice versa). Some work can be done while you do other things; schedule your time with this in mind.

TIPS FOR *Teaching*

Recast the text. We learn best by doing, by taking things apart or otherwise manipulating them to better understand how they are made, how they work. Recasting a text into a different form or perspective allows you to compare two or more versions of the same idea/subject and thereby understand why the one the author chose is (perhaps) the best approach. This approach also bolsters students' textual intelligence as they learn through such manipulations how different types of texts and elements function to shape meaning and affect the reader.

MONDAY 15

TUESDAY 16

WEDNESDAY 17

TIPS FOR *Professional Learning*

SPEND TIME. Spend time with yourself, your children, your partner, your parents. Spend time thinking, laughing, learning. Spend the wealth of your time seeing all the good movies, taking advantage of the matinee prices and the discount theater tickets. Spend time in nature. Spend your time wisely; it's your life.

practice

Weekly Reflections

On a scale of 1–10, gauge (a) *how effective you were as a teacher this week, and* (b) *how you are feeling this week*. What adjective might best capture your teaching and your feelings this week?

THURSDAY 18

FRIDAY 19

REMINDERS · NOTES · WEEKEND HOMEWORK

plan ahead

- How does next week relate to this week?
- What continues to confuse or frustrate your students?
- Think of your class as a story: What should happen next?
- Who can help you be more successful next week?

PERSONAL

WEEKLY FOCUS:

WEEKLY GOAL:

PROFESSIONAL

WEEKLY FOCUS:

WEEKLY GOAL:

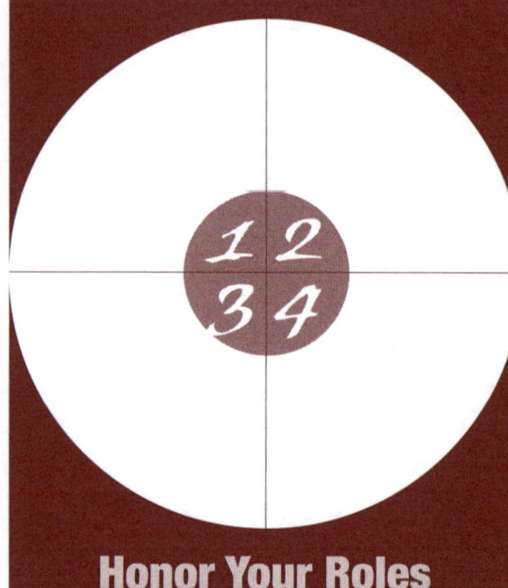

Honor Your Roles

TIPS FOR *Teachers*

Don't procrastinate. The work will not go away and create some magical opening for you to grade those papers. Use rubrics or other means of providing quick, useful feedback. Give students completion grades if necessary so you can get the papers back to them. Your own kids need your attention and your students need you to be healthy and happy and fully engaged, not burned out and resentful.

TIPS FOR *Teaching*

Read a variety of texts for different purposes. A quick skim of most contemporary magazines and newspapers (not to mention websites) reminds us how many types of text there are. And students need to know how to read them all; each one requires a different set of skills, capacities, or attitudes. Thus, we must make room for these different types of text in our curriculum, no matter what subject we teach, and, ideally, we should use them for different purposes.

MONDAY 22

TUESDAY 23

WEDNESDAY 24

The Teacher's Daybook by Jim Burke (Heinemann: Portsmouth, NH); © 2012 by Jim Burke.

TIPS FOR *Professional Learning*

GO TO INTERESTING PLACES. Every town and area has its own wealth of interesting places. Some are historical sites, others are natural wonders. Some are exciting, while others are relaxing. There are other places one might visit: retreat centers, monasteries, hostels. It can be a rich experience to take a trip to different interesting places that relate to your teaching. Take a trip through the Gold Rush territory or Civil War region, to a favorite author's town or an artist's hometown where his or her work is honored.

Weekly Reflections

On a scale of 1–10, gauge (a) *how effective you were as a teacher this week, and* (b) *how you are feeling this week*. What adjective might best capture your teaching and your feelings this week?

THURSDAY 25

FRIDAY 26

REMINDERS · NOTES · WEEKEND HOMEWORK

plan ahead

- How does next week relate to this week?
- What continues to confuse or frustrate your students?
- Think of your class as a story: What should happen next?
- Who can help you be more successful next week?

Appendices

YEAR

AUGUST	SEPTEMBER	OCTOBER	NOVEMBER	DECEMBER	JANUARY
1					
2					
3					
4					
5					
6					
7					
8					
9					
10					
11					
12					
13					
14					
15					
16					
17					
18					
19					
20					
21					
22					
23					
24					
25					
26					
27					
28					
29					
30					
31					

FEBRUARY	MARCH	APRIL	MAY	JUNE	JULY
1					
2					
3					
4					
5					
6					
7					
8					
9					
10					
11					
12					
13					
14					
15					
16					
17					
18					
19					
20					
21					
22					
23					
24					
25					
26					
27					
28					
29					
30					
31					

1. Who You Were

Use the diagram to identify all the different roles you played in your personal life (e.g., spouse, child, parent, etc.).

2. Rank the different roles from most (1) to least (10) important.

3. What You Wanted: Write your personal goal statement

This year I wanted to . . .

____

____

____

4. Why You Wanted It: Provide a rationale

I wanted to achieve this goal so that I could . . .

____

____

____

5. How You Did/Did Not Achieve It: Evaluate a plan

I did/did not reach my goal for three reasons:

1. _____________________________________

2. _____________________________________

3. _____________________________________

6. What Helped You: Identify allies and resources

The following helped me achieve my goal:

PEOPLE

1. _____________________________________

2. _____________________________________

3. _____________________________________

BOOKS

1. _____________________________________

2. _____________________________________

3. _____________________________________

ORGS/OTHER

1. _____________________________________

2. _____________________________________

3. _____________________________________

7. Assessment

I know I did/did not reach my goal because . . .

____

____

Books I Read

1. _____________________________________

2. _____________________________________

3. _____________________________________

Experiences I Had

1. _____________________________________

2. _____________________________________

3. _____________________________________

4. _____________________________________

5. _____________________________________

Places I Went/People I Saw

1. _____________________________________

2. _____________________________________

3. _____________________________________

4. _____________________________________

5. _____________________________________

Things I Did More

1. _____________________________________

2. _____________________________________

3. _____________________________________

4. _____________________________________

5. _____________________________________

Things I Did Less (or Stopped Doing)

1. _____________________________________

2. _____________________________________

3. _____________________________________

4. _____________________________________

5. _____________________________________

Things I Learned About

1. _____________________________________

2. _____________________________________

3. _____________________________________

4. _____________________________________

5. _____________________________________

If I retired tomorrow, I would spend my time . . .

____

____

1. Who You Were

Use the diagram to identify all the different roles you played in your professional life this year (e.g., teacher, coach, mentor, etc.).

2. Rank the different roles from most (1) to least (10) important.

3. What You Wanted: Write your professional goal statement

This year I wanted to . . .

____

____

4. Why You Wanted It: Provide a rationale

I wanted to achieve this goal so that I could . . .

____

____

5. How You Did/Did Not Achieve It: Evaluate a plan

I did/did not reach my goal for three reasons:

1. ______________________________________

2. ______________________________________

3. ______________________________________

6. What Helped You: Identify allies and resources

The following helped me achieve my goal:

PEOPLE
1. ______________________________________
2. ______________________________________
3. ______________________________________

BOOKS
1. ______________________________________
2. ______________________________________
3. ______________________________________

ORGS/OTHER
1. ______________________________________
2. ______________________________________
3. ______________________________________

7. Assessment

I know I did/did not reach my goal because . . .

____

____

Professional Books I Read

1. ______________________________________
2. ______________________________________
3. ______________________________________

Professional Experiences I Had

1. ______________________________________
2. ______________________________________
3. ______________________________________
4. ______________________________________

New Subjects or Texts I Taught

1. ______________________________________
2. ______________________________________
3. ______________________________________
4. ______________________________________

Contributions I Made

1. ______________________________________
2. ______________________________________
3. ______________________________________
4. ______________________________________

Things I Did Less (or Stopped Doing)

1. ______________________________________
2. ______________________________________
3. ______________________________________
4. ______________________________________

Things I Learned About

1. ______________________________________
2. ______________________________________
3. ______________________________________
4. ______________________________________

Write your own job description (based on the teacher you were):

____

____

Use this checklist to set up your class at the beginning of the school year. Use it to evaluate your room and teaching periodically throughout the school year.

Physical Environment

Basic Supplies

❏ Stapler (and staples)
❏ Tape/dispenser
❏ Paper clips
❏ Index cards
❏ Sticky notes
❏ Pens and pencils
❏ Art supplies
❏ Scissors
❏ Overhead transparencies
❏ Overhead pens
❏ Paper: computer, butcher, binder, construction
❏ Recordable CDs
❏ Chalk or whiteboard pens
❏ Yardsticks and rulers
❏ Map(s)

Technological Equipment

❏ Computer
❏ Projection device (monitor/LCD)
❏ Printer (a quiet one!)
❏ Speakers
❏ Internet connection
❏ Overhead projector
❏ Tape recorder (portable) with earphones
❏ Television
❏ Extra printer ink cartridges
❏ VCR/DVD player
❏ Camera (digital, video, or 35 mm)
❏ Stereo

Physical Space

❏ Bulletin boards to post student work and announcements
❏ Communal board for students to use
❏ Classroom library bookcases
❏ Conferencing space
❏ Regular chairs that can be moved around
❏ Podium or music stand

Organizational Space

❏ In/Out boxes
❏ Place for extra copies of handouts
❏ Clipboard(s)
❏ Bulletin/cork board

Storage Space (ideally lockable)

❏ For works-in-progress
❏ For portfolios or writing folders
❏ For art supplies
❏ For computer supplies
❏ For your personal things

Academic Supplies

❏ Good dictionaries (appropriate to grade level)
❏ ESL dictionary
❏ Bilingual dictionaries
❏ Calculator
❏ Thesaurus
❏ *Write Source 2008* (Great Source)
❏ Encyclopedia (appropriate to grade level)
❏ *The Reader's Handbook* (Great Source)

Procedural Information

❏ Students' names
❏ Contact information (for *both* parents)
❏ Special or medical needs identified (keep easily accessible)
❏ Student identification numbers
❏ Complete Substitute Information sheet
❏ Complete Teacher's Homepage

Emotional Environment

❏ Policies posted, clearly explained, consistently enforced: rules by which we live and work while in this room

❏ How do you address possible offense caused by some works (e.g., *Huck Finn*)?
❏ Check room regularly for offensive graffiti on desks or walls.
❏ How do you handle the student who says he/she "can't" or "won't" read a particular book?
❏ Do *all* students, regardless of race, gender, ability, or wealth, feel respected and comfortable in your classroom?
❏ Do students feel safe—emotionally and physically—in your class?
❏ What do you do when/if a student offends or attacks another member of the class?
❏ What do students get to make choices about in your class?
❏ Can students describe you/your class as "fair" when it comes to grading and discipline policies and their enforcement?

Intellectual Environment

❏ Do you have a significant classroom library with a range of authors, reading levels, subjects, genres?
❏ Are students confident that what they think matters and is learned in your class?
❏ In your class is there only one right answer to the questions you ask?
❏ Who asks the questions in your class?
❏ Do students have, when possible, a variety of ways to demonstrate what they know?
❏ Does your class allow for and validate different views and opinions?
❏ Do your ways of assessing students challenge them to think, or try to "catch" them?

Personal Environment

❏ Is this "your" room or "our" room?
❏ Can students meet in or otherwise use your room before school, during recess/lunch, after school?

    The Teacher's Daybook by Jim Burke (Heinemann: Portsmouth, NH); © 2012 by Jim Burke.

Name of class or student(s) ____

YOUR NOTES	DESCRIPTION OF STEPS
	1. Define the problem. Write the problem in language that is clear, specific, and concise. Focus on what a student or class does not do or understand, something that prevents their success.
	2. Generate possible causes. List all the possible causes or sources of this problem; include even those that seem not to apply but with other students might.
	3. Describe desired behavior or outcome. Provide a precise description of the behavior or action the student must show or do to succeed in the situation (e.g., your class, this assignment).
	4. Identify possible obstacles to success. Choose from the following: commitment, knowledge, skills, stamina, adaptability, elasticity. If these don't help, generate your own.
	5. Determine necessary resources. List resources—people, materials, facilities—you need to effectively help the student make the necessary changes. "Resources" do *not* include info, lessons, or skills they must learn.
	6. Identify the necessary knowledge. What do *you* need to know and believe to help this student succeed? What does the student need to know and believe to be able to succeed? What's the best way to learn this?

Use this planner to think beyond the current year to aniticipate such future events as your children's graduation years, your retirement, or proposed major vacations. On the other side, consider professional events for which you can and should plan.

PERSONAL PLANS	PROFESSIONAL PLANS
2012	
2013	
2014	
2015	
2016	
2017	
2018	
2019	
2020	

Use this planner to set deadlines for personal/professional projects to make sure that they get done. Use it as an advanced planner to note when you should begin your novel, take your trip, be ready for the state tests, or sign your kids up for summer camp.

2013	2014
January	
February	
March	
April	
May	
June	
July	
August	
September	
October	
November	
December	

BEFORE: Instructional Design

Effective instruction requires a purpose and meaningful context that etablishes not only what but why students must learn the assigned materials. Rationales such as "To meet the standards" or "To pass the test" lack meaning and do not motivate.

✔ **CONTENT STANDARDS** *What should students know and be able to do by the end of this task, unit, or course?*

Considerations

❑ Connections to previous and future skills and concepts

❑ Constraints of time and recources

❑ Availability of necessary materials and resources

✔ **STUDENT PREPARATION** *What should students know and be able to do to accomplish Content Standards goals?*

Considerations

❑ Specialized or new vocabulary terms

❑ Background knowledge on the idea, historical period, or story

❑ Skills, habits, capacities, or techniques

❑ Connections to previously learned skills and concepts

✔ **TEACHER PREPARATION** *What skills, knowledge, or resources does the teacher need to effectively teach this skill or concept?*

Considerations

❑ What the teacher needs or wants to teach after this unit

❑ What support or material resources are available to help teach this skill or concept?

✔ **INSTRUCTIONAL STANDARDS** *What strategies and instructional designs are most effective and efficient in teaching this skill or concept?*

Considerations

❑ Graphic organizers

❑ Notetaking strategies

❑ Instructional strategies: reciprocal teaching, literature circles, direct instruction

❑ Class and student configurations (e.g., pairs, groups, whole class)

❑ Visual aids, multimodal, multisensory approaches

✔ **CURRICULAR CONVERSATIONS** *How does this skill or concept relate to the larger themes in the course, curriculum, or lives of students?*

Considerations

❑ Workplace connections

❑ Personal connections

❑ Cross-curricular connections

✔ **STANDARDS ALIGNMENT** *Which standard(s) will this task or unit help students master?*

Considerations

❑ Curricular objectives and context of the lesson

❑ Current progress toward mastery of this standard

❑ Connections to and reinforcement of standards students have already met

❑ Standards you have not yet addressed or which students have not yet mastered

❑ Extent to which this task or unit prepares students to meet other standards, for example, district frameworks, ESLRs, Advanced Placement, exit exam, or SAT standards

✔ **PERFORMANCE STANDARDS** *What evidence of student learning or mastery are you willing to accept?*

Considerations

❑ Is there more than one way to show mastery of this skill or concept?

❑ Do students have ample opportunity and means by which to master this standard?

❑ Do students know what a successful performance looks like (e.g., through exemplars or modeling)?

❑ Do students know the criteria by which their performance will be evaluated up front (e.g., through exemplars, rubrics, directions, modeling)?

❑ Are the criteria for mastery consistent with those in other classes, schools, districts, and states?

❑ Are all skills and concepts equally important—and given equal weight—on all assessments?

❑ Is this method an effective and appropriate use of the teacher's time and attention?

DURING: Implementation and Experience

Effective design demands that we lay a solid but adaptable foundation that will ensure the success of the task or unit once it begins. While such attention to design asks a lot of the teacher at first, such questions and considerations become mental habits that lead to efficient and effective instructional design.

✔ **TEACHING AND LEARNING**   *This list offers a sequence of steps that build on learners' knowledge and progress by extending their capacity and competence as they move toward mastery of a standard:*

Considerations

❏ *Introduce* the skill, concept, or task with clear instructions that students can hear, see, and read.

❏ *Connect* the task, concept, or unit to what they have studied or will study.

❏ *Assess* prior knowledge and current understanding of the skill or concept.

❏ *Demonstrate* the task, explaining what you are thinking as you do so.

❏ *Try* the task or explain their initial understanding of the concept.

❏ *Evaluate* their performance; check for understanding.

❏ *Correct* or clarify their performance as needed, based on observed results.

❏ *Practice* the skill or continue study of the concept.

❏ *Assess* level of mastery and need for further group or individualized instruction.

❏ *Extend* students' understanding and mastery by increasing the difficulty of the task.

❏ *Monitor* students' level of mastery and need for further group or individualized instruction.

❏ *Reinforce* understanding and mastery as you move on to next task or concept.

AFTER: Evaluation and Planning

Feedback and reinforcement are essential elements in any instructional design. In this last stage, teachers answer the question "What next?" before returning to the beginning and starting the process with a new task or concept.

✔ **INSTRUCTIONAL STANDARDS**   *What does the performance data tell you the students need to do or learn next?*

Considerations

❏ Did all students master the skill or concept?

❏ What is the next step—and why?

❏ Was your method the most effective means to teach this skill or concept?

❏ What changes should you make in the technique or assignment next time?

✔ **WHAT'S NEXT**   *Return to the beginning and follow the sequence for teaching the next skill or concept.*

Daily Lesson Planner

CLASS

DATE   PERIOD

TODAY I WANT MY STUDENTS TO . . .

MY WEEKLY GOAL IS . . .

TEACH BY DESIGN

BEFORE *Did you:*
- ❏ consider students' prior knowledge and experience?
- ❏ establish the assessment criteria?
- ❏ provide models to help students understand the task?
- ❏ connect today's lesson with previous learning and other disciplines?
- ❏ give effective oral and written directions?
- ❏ consider students' backgrounds, interests, and cognitive development?
- ❏ establish and communicate goals?
- ❏ choose the appropriate strategy and tools for optimum learning?

DURING *Did you:*
- ❏ use a variety of instructional strategies and resources?
- ❏ provide opportunities for students to assess their own learning?
- ❏ treat all students with respect and fairness?
- ❏ encourage all students to participate?
- ❏ enforce expectations for behavior fairly and consistently?
- ❏ employ instructional strategies appropriate to the subject matter?
- ❏ use materials, resources, and technologies to make subject matter accessible to students?
- ❏ allow students to practice before working independently?
- ❏ follow a logical sequence?

AFTER *Did you:*
- ❏ use multiple forms of assessment?
- ❏ consider short- and long-term learning needs?
- ❏ use assessment results to guide instruction?
- ❏ give students time to begin homework so you can be sure they understand?
- ❏ clarify homework directions and due date?

FOCUS ON STUDENTS:

RESOURCES NEEDED:

STANDARDS TAUGHT:

THE FIRST FIVE MINUTES   READ • TAKE ROLL • REVIEW • ASSESS • RETURN/COLLECT WORK • ANNOUNCE

THE FINAL FIVE MINUTES   READ • REVIEW • ASSESS • BEGIN/RETURN WORK • DISCUSS • DIRECTIONS

REFLECTION: WHAT DID/DID NOT WORK? WHAT WERE YOU TRYING TO ACCOMPLISH? WHAT HAPPENED?

<table>
<tr><td colspan="2" rowspan="2"># Essential Lessons Template</td><td>CLASS</td><td>PERIOD</td><td>DATE</td></tr>
<tr><td>LESSON</td><td></td><td></td></tr>
</table>

PLANNING

FRAME THE LESSON   Position the lesson within your curriculum and your students' academic needs.

ESSENTIAL SKILL SET   List specific instructional activities.

GATHER AND PREPARE   List the resources you'll need and suggestions for adapting the lesson for your students.

TEACHING

- develop instructional language, moves, and prompts
- subdivide the lesson
- identify discussion topics
- provide tangible and concrete examples

ASSESSING

- list strategies to provide extra support or extra challenge
- assess understanding of lesson
- reinforce and extend lesson

FRAME THE LESSON

GATHER AND PREPARE

TEACH

ASSESS AND EXTEND

NOTES

Use this page to orient yourself. Effective curriculum design requires both micro and macro planning. If you cut straight to the obvious and all-important question, "What am I doing on the first day?" you might preclude certain options later on. Use this page to help you figure out the questions your curriculum is trying to answer—and ask. Use the Planning Prompts to remind or guide you; or create your own Planning Page with your own prompts and reminders. Its primary purpose is to help you establish, remember, and accomplish the goals you (and your department, district, or state) set when you sat down to decide what and how students will learn. For more specific planning help, see Designing a Standards-Based Curriculum.

Planning Prompts

- By the end of the first period (of this assignment, unit, or class), students should . . .
- By the end of the first week (of this assignment, unit, or class), students should . . .
- By the end of the first month (of this assignment, unit, or class), students should . . .
- By the end of the semester, students should . . .
- By the end of the first year, students should . . .

COURSE		DATE(S)	
WHAT	**WHEN**	**WHY**	**HOW**

ASSESS YOURSELF IN EACH CLASS USING THIS SCALE: 1 = ALWAYS | 2 = USUALLY | 3 = SOMETIMES | 4 = RARELY | 5 = NEVER

ACADEMIC HABITS	1°	2°	3°	4°	5°	6°	7°	Total
1. I ask for help if I do not understand something.								
2. I bring *all* the necessary supplies.								
3. I bring my textbook.								
4. I check my work before I turn it in to make sure it satisfies all the requirements and is my "best work."								
5. I come to class on time.								
6. I complete all homework.								
7. I have a dedicated place where I do my homework.								
8. I keep my student ID card with me at all times.								
9. I keep old assignments, quizzes, and tests until the semester ends (to review and to prove my grades).								
10. I keep track of my standing in each class.								
11. I listen to what the teacher and other students say.								
12. I organize all notes and materials in a binder with section dividers that are labeled.								
13. I participate in full-class discussions.								
14. I participate in small-group discussions.								
15. I read all the directions before taking tests or doing assignments.								
16. I review my tests/assignments after I get them back.								
17. I set aside specific time for doing homework.								
18. I set goals and make plans to help me achieve them.								
19. I study before all quizzes and exams.								
20. I take notes during lectures, discussions, or videos.								
21. I take notes when I read the assigned readings.								
22. I use a planner to keep track of events/assignments.								
23. I use specific strategies and aids to understand and remember information.								
24. I use specific strategies to help me do my work well and focus my attention.								
25. I write down the homework assignments.								

Grand Total ________

Estimated (current) letter grade in this class __________

1. In _______________________ (favorite/strongest class) my teacher would say I am:

    1. __________________   2. __________________   3. __________________

2. In _______________________ (least favorite/hardest class) my teacher would say I am:

    1. __________________   2. __________________   3. __________________

3. Reflective Essay

Using the information (your scores) and words from above, write a 1–2 page reflection on the type of student you are and would like to be. Discuss those things you do well and those areas you need to improve to become an even better student. Be sure to provide examples and discuss them as they relate to the ideas in your paper.

The Four Cs of Academic Success

COMMITMENT

Commitment describes the extent to which students care about the work and maintain consistency in their attempt to succeed.

Key aspects of **commitment** are:

- *Emotional investment*: Refers to how much students care about their success and the quality of their work on this assignment or performance.
- *Effort*: Some students resist making a serious effort when they do not believe they can succeed. Without such effort, neither success nor improvement is possible.
- *Consistency*: Everyone can be great or make heroic efforts for a day or even a week; real, sustainable success in a class or on large assignments requires consistent hard work and "quality conscience."
- *Faith*: Students must believe that the effort they make will eventually lead to the result or success they seek. *Faith* applies to a method or means by which they hope to achieve success.
- *Permission*: Students must give themselves permission to learn and work hard and others permission to teach and support them if they are to improve and succeed.

CONTENT

Content refers to information or processes students must know to complete a task or succeed on an assignment in class.

Content knowledge includes:

- *Discipline- or subject-specific matter* such as names, concepts, and terms.
- *Cultural reference points* not specifically related to the subject but necessary to understand the material, such as:
  - People
  - Events
  - Trends
  - Ideas
  - Dates
- *Conventions* related to documents, procedures, genres, or experiences.
- *Features, cues, or other signals* that convey meaning during a process or within a text.
- *Language* needed to complete or understand the task.
- Procedures used during the course of the task or assignment.

COMPETENCIES

Competencies are those skills students need to be able to complete the assignment or succeed at some task.

Representative, general **competencies** include the ability to:

- *Generate* ideas, solutions, and interpretations that will lead to the successful completion of the task.
- *Manage* resources (time, people, and materials) needed to complete the task; refers also to the ability to govern oneself.
- *Communicate* ideas and information to complete and convey results of the work.
- *Evaluate* and *make decisions* based on information needed to complete the assignment or succeed at the task.
- *Learn* while completing the assignment so students can improve their performance on similar assignments in the future.
- *Use* a range of tools and strategies to solve the problems they encounter.

CAPACITIES

Capacities account for the quantifiable aspects of performance; students can have great skills but lack the capacity to fully employ those skills.

Primary **capacities** related to academic performance include:

- *Speed* with which students can perform one or more tasks needed to complete the assignment or performance.
- *Stamina* required to maintain the requisite level of performance; includes physical and mental stamina.
- *Fluency* needed to handle problems or interpret ideas that vary from students' past experience or learning.
- *Dexterity*, which allows students, when needed, to do more than one task at the same time (a.k.a. multitasking).
- *Memory* so students can draw on useful background information or store information needed for subsequent tasks included in the assignment.
- *Resiliency* needed to persevere despite initial or periodic obstacles to success on the assignment or performance.
- *Confidence* in their ideas, methods, skills, and overall abilities related to this task.

English Language Arts Anchor Standards, 6–12

College and Career Readiness Anchor Standards for Reading

The grades 6–12 standards on the following pages define what students should understand and be able to do by the end of each grade. They correspond to the College and Career Readiness (CCR) anchor standards below by number. The CCR and grade-specific standards are necessary complements—the former providing broad standards, the latter providing additional specificity—that together define the skills and understandings that all students must demonstrate.

Key Ideas and Details

1. Read closely to determine what the text says explicitly and to make logical inferences from it; cite specific textual evidence when writing or speaking to support conclusions drawn from the text.
2. Determine central ideas or themes of a text and analyze their development; summarize the key supporting details and ideas.
3. Analyze how and why individuals, events, and ideas develop and interact over the course of a text.

Craft and Structure

4. Interpret words and phrases as they are used in a text, including determining technical, connotative, and figurative meanings, and analyze how specific word choices shape meaning or tone.
5. Analyze the structure of texts, including how specific sentences, paragraphs, and larger portions of the text (e.g., a section, chapter, scene, or stanza) relate to each other and the whole.

6. Assess how point of view or purpose shapes the content and style of a text.

Integration of Knowledge and Ideas

7. Integrate and evaluate content presented in diverse formats and media, including visually and quantitatively, as well as in words.
8. Delineate and evaluate the argument and specific claims in a text, including the validity of the reasoning as well as the relevance and sufficiency of the evidence.
9. Analyze how two or more texts address similar themes or topics in order to build knowledge or to compare the approaches the authors take.

Range of Reading and Level of Text Complexity

10. Read and comprehend complex literary and informational texts independently and proficiently.

Note on range and content of student reading

To become college and career ready, students must grapple with works of exceptional craft and thought whose range extends across genres, cultures, and centuries. Such works offer profound insights into the human condition and serve as models for students' own thinking and writing. Along with high-quality contemporary works, these texts should be chosen from among seminal U.S. documents, the classics of American literature, and the timeless dramas of Shakespeare. Through wide and deep reading of literature and literary nonfiction of steadily increasing sophistication, students gain a reservoir of literary and cultural knowledge, references, and images; the ability to evaluate intricate arguments; and the capacity to surmount the challenges posed by complex texts.

College and Career Readiness Anchor Standards for Writing

The grades 6–12 standards on the following pages define what students should understand and be able to do by the end of each grade. They correspond to the College and Career Readiness (CCR) anchor standards below by number. The CCR and grade-specific standards are necessary complements—the former providing broad standards, the latter providing additional specificity—that together define the skills and understandings that all students must demonstrate.

Text Types and Purposes

1. Write arguments to support claims in an analysis of substantive topics or texts, using valid reasoning and relevant and sufficient evidence.
2. Write informative/explanatory texts to examine and convey complex ideas and information clearly and accurately through the effective selection, organization, and analysis of content.
3. Write narratives to develop real or imagined experiences or events using effective technique, well-chosen details, and well-structured event sequences.

Production and Distribution of Writing

4. Produce clear and coherent writing in which the development, organization, and style are appropriate to task, purpose, and audience.
5. Develop and strengthen writing as needed by planning, revising, editing, rewriting, or trying a new approach.

6. Use technology, including the Internet, to produce and publish writing and to interact and collaborate with others.

Research to Build and Present Knowledge

7. Conduct short as well as more sustained research projects based on focused questions, demonstrating understanding of the subject under investigation.
8. Gather relevant information from multiple print and digital sources, assess the credibility and accuracy of each source, and integrate the information while avoiding plagiarism.
9. Draw evidence from literary or informational texts to support analysis, reflection, and research.

Range of Writing

10. Write routinely over extended time frames (time for research, reflection, and revision) and shorter time frames (a single sitting or a day or two) for a range of tasks, purposes, and audiences.

The Teacher's Daybook by Jim Burke (Heinemann: Portsmouth, NH); © 2012 by Jim Burke.

Note on range and content of student writing

For students, writing is a key means of asserting and defending claims, showing what they know about a subject, and conveying what they have experienced, imagined, thought, and felt. To be college- and career-ready writers, students must take task, purpose, and audience into careful consideration, choosing words, information, structures, and formats deliberately. They need to know how to combine elements of different kinds of writing—for example, to use narrative strategies within argument and explanation within narrative—to produce complex and nuanced writing. They need to be able to use technology strategically when creating, refining, and collaborating on writing. They have to become adept at gathering information, evaluating sources, and citing material accurately, reporting findings from their research and analysis of sources in a clear and cogent manner. They must have the flexibility, concentration, and fluency to produce high-quality first-draft text under a tight deadline as well as the capacity to revisit and make improvements to a piece of writing over multiple drafts when circumstances encourage or require it.

College and Career Readiness Anchor Standards for Speaking and Listening

The grades 6–12 standards on the following pages define what students should understand and be able to do by the end of each grade. They correspond to the College and Career Readiness (CCR) anchor standards below by number. The CCR and grade-specific standards are necessary complements—the former providing broad standards, the latter providing additional specificity—that together define the skills and understandings that all students must demonstrate.

Comprehension and Collaboration

1. Prepare for and participate effectively in a range of conversations and collaborations with diverse partners, building on others' ideas and expressing their own clearly and persuasively.
2. Integrate and evaluate information presented in diverse media and formats, including visually, quantitatively, and orally.
3. Evaluate a speaker's point of view, reasoning, and use of evidence and rhetoric.

Presentation of Knowledge and Ideas

4. Present information, findings, and supporting evidence such that listeners can follow the line of reasoning and the organization, development, and style are appropriate to task, purpose, and audience.
5. Make strategic use of digital media and visual displays of data to express information and enhance understanding of presentations.
6. Adapt speech to a variety of contexts and communicative tasks, demonstrating command of formal English when indicated or appropriate.

Note on range and content of student speaking and listening

To become college and career ready, students must have ample opportunities to take part in a variety of rich, structured conversations—as part of a whole class, in small groups, and with a partner—built around important content in various domains. They must be able to contribute appropriately to these conversations, to make comparisons and contrasts, and to analyze and synthesize a multitude of ideas in accordance with the standards of evidence appropriate to a particular discipline. Whatever their intended major or profession, high school graduates will depend heavily on their ability to listen attentively to others so that they are able to build on others' meritorious ideas while expressing their own clearly and persuasively.

New technologies have broadened and expanded the role that speaking and listening play in acquiring and sharing knowledge and have tightened their link to other forms of communication. The Internet has accelerated the speed at which connections between speaking, listening, reading, and writing can be made, requiring that students be ready to use these modalities nearly simultaneously. Technology itself is changing quickly, creating a new urgency for students to be adaptable in response to change.

The Teacher's Daybook by Jim Burke (Heinemann: Portsmouth, NH); © 2012 by Jim Burke.

College and Career Readiness Anchor Standards for Language

The grades 6–12 standards on the following pages define what students should understand and be able to do by the end of each grade. They correspond to the College and Career Readiness (CCR) anchor standards below by number. The CCR and grade-specific standards are necessary complements—the former providing broad standards, the latter providing additional specificity—that together define the skills and understandings that all students must demonstrate.

Conventions of Standard English

1. Demonstrate command of the conventions of standard English grammar and usage when writing or speaking.
2. Demonstrate command of the conventions of standard English capitalization, punctuation, and spelling when writing.

Knowledge of Language

3. Apply knowledge of language to understand how language functions in different contexts, to make effective choices for meaning or style, and to comprehend more fully when reading or listening.

Vocabulary Acquisition and Use

4. Determine or clarify the meaning of unknown and multiple-meaning words and phrases by using context clues, analyzing meaningful word parts, and consulting general and specialized reference materials, as appropriate.
5. Demonstrate understanding of word relationships and nuances in word meanings.
6. Acquire and use accurately a range of general academic and domain-specific words and phrases sufficient for reading, writing, speaking, and listening at the college and career readiness level; demonstrate independence in gathering vocabulary knowledge when considering a word or phrase important to comprehension or expression.

Note on range and content of student language use

To be college and career ready in language, students must have firm control over the conventions of standard English. At the same time, they must come to appreciate that language is as at least as much a matter of craft as of rules and be able to choose words, syntax, and punctuation to express themselves and achieve particular functions and rhetorical effects. They must also have extensive vocabularies, built through reading and study, enabling them to comprehend complex texts and engage in purposeful writing about and conversations around content. They need to become skilled in determining or clarifying the meaning of words and phrases they encounter, choosing flexibly from an array of strategies to aid them. They must learn to see an individual word as part of a network of other words—words, for example, that have similar denotations but different connotations. The inclusion of Language standards in their own strand should not be taken as an indication that skills related to conventions, effective language use, and vocabulary are unimportant to reading, writing, speaking, and listening; indeed, they are inseparable from such contexts.

Substitute Information Template

Teacher's Name ________________________________   Date(s) Absent ________________________________

SUGGESTIONS: Set up a two-pocket folder. Write "Sub Plans" and your name on the cover. Inside, stock it with forms, passes, and information listed below. Keep this in an easily found place in case you need to phone in substitute plans; that way you can say, "It's in my top right-hand drawer."

Schedule

PER	CLASS	LOCATION	AIDE/VOLUNTEER	HELPFUL STUDENTS	HELPFUL TEACHER
1°					
2°					
3°					
4°					
5°					
6°					
7°					

Essential Information

TO FIND:	LOOK:
Today's lessons plans	
Roll book	
Bell schedule	
Hall pass	
Assignments/handouts/video	
School policies/map	
Daily bulletin/announcements	
Referral slips	
Emergency information/supplies	
Supplies (pens, chalk, paper, etc.)	
Keys to ________________	
Teacher's edition of textbooks	
Seating charts	
Classroom activity schedule	
TV/DVD remote controls	

Troubleshooting

IF YOU HAVE:	CALL/SEND TO:	PHONE/ROOM NUMBER
Discipline problems		
Medical emergency		
Audiovisual equipment trouble		
Copies to make		
To go to the bathroom		
A kid who wants to use the computer		
A state (or some other such) test		
Students with personal problems		

    The Teacher's Daybook by Jim Burke (Heinemann: Portsmouth, NH); © 2012 by Jim Burke.

Teacher ____

Class _________________ Semester ________________

Period __________ Room ____________________________

155

STUDENT NAME																					
1.																					
2.																					
3.																					
4.																					
5.																					
6.																					
7.																					
8.																					
9.																					
10.																					
11.																					
12.																					
13.																					
14.																					
15.																					
16.																					
17.																					
18.																					
19.																					
20.																					
21.																					
22.																					
23.																					
24.																					
25.																					
26.																					
27.																					
28.																					
29.																					
30.																					
31.																					
32.																					
33.																					
34.																					
35.																					
36.																					
37.																					
38.																					
39.																					

Date

TIME	PERSON • PLACE • EVENT

NAME	NUMBER

THINGS TO DO

Month	Dates	Year

MONDAY	Remember	Morning	Afternoon	Evening

TUESDAY	Remember	Morning	Afternoon	Evening

WEDNESDAY	Remember	Morning	Afternoon	Evening

THURSDAY	Remember	Morning	Afternoon	Evening

FRIDAY	Remember	Morning	Afternoon	Evening

SATURDAY	Remember	Morning	Afternoon	Evening

SUNDAY	Remember	Morning	Afternoon	Evening

Use this page to reflect on not only your personal and professional needs, but your students' needs, also. Assess your life at home and at work to discover which needs you are and are not meeting for yourself, your family, your students, and colleagues.

NEEDS	NOTES

1. **Comfort:** Having enough to eat and drink, keeping warm when it's cool and cool when it's warm, being free from pain.

2. **Safety:** Feeling secure in your surroundings, being protected from crime, surviving accidents and natural disasters, having an environment free of pollutants.

3. **Control:** Having a hand in your own destiny, planning for the future, fixing things and people, influencing or directing others, controlling your environment.

4. **Tradition:** Having a sense of roots, having a feeling of continuity with the past, doing things as they have always been done, honoring your forbears.

5. **Friendship:** Establishing warm relations with others, being a member of a group or organization, being accepted by others, having someone to love and be loved by.

6. **Nurturance:** Taking care of others, comforting those in distress, aiding the helpless, caring for animals, giving to charitable organizations, providing volunteer service.

7. **Recognition:** Being treated as valuable and important, having your achievements praised by others, receiving trophies or awards, being the center of attention.

8. **Success:** Accomplishing something of significance, overcoming obstacles to achieve your goals, doing better than expected, reaching the pinnacle of your profession.

9. **Independence:** Being able to stand on your own, being self-sufficient, making your own decisions, being your own person.

10. **Variety:** Longing for adventure, visiting new and unusual places, trying different things, changing jobs, moving to a new town, meeting new people.

11. **Curiosity:** Understanding the world around you, understanding yourself, understanding others, questioning why things happen or why people act as they do, finding out about the unusual.

12. **Enjoyment:** Doing something just for the fun of it, taking a vacation, pampering yourself, pursuing a hobby.

(Source: Michael Osborn and Suzanne Osborn, *Public Speaking, Fourth Edition*. Copyright © 1997 by Houghton Mifflin Company. Reprinted with permission.)

Use this page to keep track of birthdays, anniversaries, and other recurring events in your personal life. Use it to organize all testing dates and other such professional events in one place for easy reference.

PERSONAL DATES	
DATE	EVENT

PROFESSIONAL DATES	
DATE	EVENT

Professional Portfolio Page

DIRECTIONS: Use this to keep a record of professional confer-ences, committee meetings, workshops, classes, or any other experiences appropriate for your resume, professional growth record, or teacher evaluation.

Teacher ___________________________

Year _____________ Department _____________

✔	DATE	EVENT/ACTION	LOCATION	PROVIDER	HOURS	COST/PAY	DESCRIPTION/NOTE

NOTES

Recommended Reading and Works Cited

Allen, Janet. 1995. *It's Never Too Late: Leading Adolescents to Lifelong Literacy*. Portsmouth, NH: Heinemann.

Bradley, Bill. 1998. *Values of the Game.* New York: Broadway.

Burke, Jim. 2012. *The English Teacher's Companion: A Complete Guide to Curriculum, Classroom, and the Profession.* Fourth Edition. Portsmouth, NH: Heinemann.

———. 2000. *Reading Reminders: Tools, Tips, and Techniques.* Portsmouth, NH: Heinemann.

———. 2002. *The Reader's Handbook: A Student Guide for Reading and Learning.* Wilmington, MA: Great Source.

———. 2002. *Tools for Thought: Helping All Students Read, Write, and Think.* Portsmouth, NH: Heinemann.

———. 2006. *Letters to a New Teacher: A Month-by-Month Guide to the Year Ahead.* Portsmouth, NH: Heinemann.

Codell, Esmé Raji. 1999. *Educating Esmé: Diary of a Teacher's First Year.* Chapel Hill, NC: Algonquin.

Covey, Stephen R. 1989. *The Seven Habits of Highly Effective People: Restoring the Character Ethic.* New York: Simon and Schuster.

Covey, Stephen R., A. Roger Merrill, and Rebecca R. Merrill. 1994. *First Things First: To Live, to Love, to Learn, to Leave a Legacy.* New York: Fireside.

Csikszentmihalyi, Mihaly. 1990. *Flow: The Psychology of Optimal Experience.* New York: HarperPerennial.

Daloz, Laurent A. Parks, Cheryl Keen, James Keen, and Sharon Daloz Parks. 1996. *Common Fire: Leading Lives of Commitment in a Complex World.* Boston: Beacon.

Draper, Sharon M. 2000. *Teaching from the Heart: Reflections, Encouragement, and Inspiration.* Portsmouth, NH: Heinemann.

———. 2001. *Not Quite Burned Out But Crispy Around the Edges: Inspiration, Laughter, and Encouragement for Teachers.* Portsmouth, NH: Heinemann.

Fisher, Bobbi. 2000. *The Teacher Book: Finding Personal and Professional Balance.* Portsmouth, NH: Heinemann.

Fox, Matthew. 1994. *The Reinvention of Work: A New Vision of Livelihood for Our Time.* New York: Harper San Francisco.

Gayles, Gloria Wade. 2003. *In Praise of Our Teachers: A Multicultural Tribute to Those Who Inspired Us.* Boston, MA: Beacon Press.

Graves, Donald. 2001. *The Energy to Teach.* Portsmouth, NH: Heinemann.

———. 2004. *Teaching Day by Day: 180 Stories to Help You Along the Way.* Portsmouth, NH: Heinemann.

Intrator, Sam. 2002. *Stories of the Courage to Teach: Honoring the Teacher's Heart.* San Francisco: Jossey-Bass.

Intrator, Sam (ed). 2005. *Living the Questions: Essays Inspired by the Work and Life of Parker J. Palmer.* San Francisco: Jossey-Bass.

Intrator, Sam, and Megan Scribner. 2003. *Teaching with Fire: Poetry That Sustains the Courage to Teach.* San Francisco: Jossey-Bass.

———. 2007. *Leading from Within: Poetry That Sustains the Courage to Lead.* San Francisco: Jossey-Bass.

Kessler, Rachel. 2000. *The Soul of Education: Helping Students Find Connection, Compassion, and Character at School.* Alexandria, VA: Association for Supervision and Curriculum Development.

Kittle, Penny. 2003. *Public Teaching: One Kid at a Time.* Portsmouth, NH: Heinemann.

Lamott, Anne. 1994. *Bird by Bird: Some Instructions on Writing and Life.* New York: Pantheon Books.

Loehr, Jim, and Tony Schwartz. 2003. *The Power of Full Engagement: Managing Energy, Not Time, Is the Key to High Performance and Personal Renewal.* New York: Free Press.

Lundin, Stephen, Harry Paul, and John Christensen. 2000. *Fish: A Remarkable Way to Boost Morale and Improve Results.* New York: Hyperion.

Morris, Tom. 1994. *True Success: A New Philosophy of Excellence.* New York: Berkeley.

Osborn, Michael, and Suzanne Osborn. 1997. *Public Speaking,* 4/e. Boston: Houghton Mifflin.

Palmer, Parker. 1990. *The Active Life: A Spirituality of Work, Creativity, and Caring.* San Francisco: Jossey-Bass.

———. 1993. *To Know as We Are Known: Education as a Spiritual Journey.* San Francisco: Jossey-Bass.

———. 1998. *The Courage to Teach: Exploring the Inner Landscape of a Teacher's Life.* San Francisco: Jossey-Bass.

———. 2000. *Let Your Life Speak: Listening for the Voice of Vocation.* San Francisco: Jossey-Bass.

———. 2004. *A Hidden Wholeness: The Journey Toward an Undivided Life.* San Francisco: Jossey-Bass.

———. 2007. *The Courage to Teach: Exploring the Inner Landscape of a Teacher's Life.* 10th anniveray ed. San Francisco: Jossey-Bass.

Parks, Sharon Daloz. 2000. *Big Questions, Worthy Dreams: Mentoring Young Adults in Their Search for Meaning, Purpose, and Faith.* San Francisco: Jossey-Bass.

Phillips, Christopher. 2001. *Socrates Café: A Fresh Taste of Philosophy.* New York: W.W. Norton.

Routman, Regie. 1996. *Literacy at the Crossroads: Crucial Talk About Reading, Writing, and Other Teaching Dilemmas.* Portsmouth, NH: Heinemann.

Whyte, David. 2001. *Crossing the Unknown Sea: Work as a Pilgrimage of Identity.* New York: Riverhead.

Wong, Harry K., and Rosemary T. Wong. 1998. *The First Days of School: How to Be an Effective Teacher.* Mt. View, CA: Harry K. Wong.

Zander, Rosamund Stone, and Benjamin Zander. 2000. *The Art of Possibility: Transforming Professional and Personal Life.* Boston: Harvard School of Business Press.